What's to Eat?

The Milk-Free, Egg-Free, Nut-Free
Food Allergy Cookbook

Linda Marienhoff Coss

Plumtree Press

Lake Forest, California

WHAT'S TO EAT?

THE MILK-FREE, EGG-FREE, NUT-FREE FOOD
ALLERGY COOKBOOK

Plumtree Press/November, 2000

Dedication

I dedicate this book to Jason and Kevin.
May you enjoy health, peace, and joy all the days
of your lives. Eat well and be happy,
and know that I love you.

Also by Linda Coss

How To Manage Your Child's
Life-Threatening Food Allergies

Practical Tips For Everyday Life

Acknowledgements

I would like to thank my children, Jason and Kevin, for putting up with all of my kitchen experimentation; my parents and family for their unconditional love and support; Catherine Balck, recipe taster and recipe namer extraordinaire; all of my food tasters and recipe testers, including Rick Coss, Laura Blackie, Diana Marienhoff, Alex Randall, Rene Stern, Heidi Kahn, Michelle Gerstley, and more; Leslie Lawicki for her editing assistance; Robin and Art Smith, for their wonderful graphic design; and all of the members of my Food Allergy Support Group for their continuing love and support in life, whether food-allergy-related or not.

Legal Disclaimer

The information contained in this book is not intended to replace the advice of your physician, nor is it meant to replace medical diagnosis or treatment. If you have or suspect that you have food allergies, you are strongly urged to seek out appropriate medical advice. If you are already under the care of a physician for your food allergies, be sure to discuss with him or her any changes that you intend to make in your diet.

If you or someone that you are cooking for suffers from severe food allergies, it is imperative that you check the ingredient panel of each item that you use in your cooking, in order to ensure that the item does not contain any food allergens. This must be done every time that the item is purchased, as food manufacturers often change their ingredients without notice. In addition, you must be sure that any open containers of food to be used in your cooking have not been "contaminated" with a food allergen. For example, a jar of jelly which does not have any dairy, egg, or nut ingredients listed in its ingredient panel will contain peanut if at some point in time a knife that had peanut butter on it had been placed in the jelly jar; in this case, the jelly should not be eaten by a person who has peanut allergy.

No promises or warranties, express or implied, as to the appropriateness of any food or recipe for a particular person's diet is made by this book. No liability will be assumed by anyone affiliated with the writing, production or distribution of this book for any damages arising from the preparation or consumption of the foods described herein, whether such losses are special, incidental, consequential, or otherwise.

The reader accepts sole responsibility for the use of the information contained in this book.

Table of Contents

Introduction

Nine years ago my then-one-year-old son was diagnosed with severe, potentially fatal, multiple food allergies. Although it was somewhat of a relief to get an official diagnosis of my son's condition, the reality struck me as rather harsh. Jason could not eat any milk products or milk derivatives, eggs, peanuts, or tree nuts. He could not eat any foods which contained any of these things as an ingredient. In fact, Jason was so exquisitely sensitive to these allergens that he could not eat foods that had merely come in contact with something that he was allergic to. As there currently is no "cure" for food allergy, we were told that strict avoidance of the offending foods was an absolute necessity.

Strict avoidance of milk products, eggs, and nuts? That's easy for you to say, Mr. Allergy Doctor – but what am I supposed to fix for dinner? And how about breakfast, lunch, and dessert, for that matter? Just what am I supposed to feed this child? After my panic subsided, I began my journey into the world of dairy-, egg-, and nut-free cooking.

I consulted with a nutritionist. She gave me a long list of ways in which "dairy," "egg," and "nut" might be listed on ingredient panels, the address of a (then fledgling) group in Virginia called the Food Allergy Network, and advised me to give Jason calcium supplements. That's great advice, Ms. Nutritionist – but what am I supposed to fix for dinner?

I soon discovered that most of my favorite recipes contained the now-forbidden ingredients and, although I have since learned that "dairy, egg, and nut" seems to be a fairly common allergy combination among those who have multiple food allergies, I could not find a cookbook that addressed Jason's needs. Recipes that were milk-free often contained eggs, egg-free recipes often contained milk or nuts, or acceptable recipes sounded so unappealing (such as Baked Tofu Rice-and-Oat Bran Balls) that I could not bring myself to try them.

Trying to make desserts that my son could eat was an especially big challenge. I tried every dairy- and egg-free recipe for baked goods that I could get my hands on and soon found that most of these recipes had one thing in common: they were terrible! But I persevered, and eventually I resolved to write my own cookbook.

The results are in your hands. I sincerely hope that this cookbook helps you and your family to enjoy wonderful, delicious food in spite of a limited diet. While other food allergy cookbooks that you might have seen tend to focus on what I call "substitution cooking" (i.e. how to make cheesecake without cheese or soufflé without eggs), in creating the recipes that are contained in this book I have tried to focus on cooking fabulous foods that just do not happen to contain any milk products, eggs, or nuts. If cheese-less cheesecake is what you're looking for, you won't find it here. But if what you're looking for is recipes for delicious meals and desserts that you can serve to your family and guests with pride, if you don't want to feel "restricted" by a restricted diet, this book is for you.

Bon appetit!

Ingredients

One of the keys to a dairy-, egg-, and nut-free diet is learning how to recognize all of the myriad ways in which these items may be listed on the ingredient panels of the packaged foods you purchase, and then avoiding them. I realize this is easier said than done, especially with dairy products. The list of ways in which milk or milk derivatives can be listed on an ingredient panel is dauntingly long, and milk products seem to show up in a large percentage of packaged foods on the market today. But let me assure you, label-reading does get easier with practice!

Because severe food allergies can be life-threatening, for some people (such as my son), a "strict avoidance" diet can mean the difference between an enjoyable meal and an ambulance ride to the emergency room. If you must completely avoid all milk, egg, and nut ingredients, it is **imperative that you check the ingredient panel of each item that you purchase**, including items that are to be used as ingredients in your cooking, **each time you purchase them**. *If you are not sure if an item is "safe," do not eat it!*

If you are exquisitely sensitive to particular foods, you must also watch out for the "cross-contamination" that can occur when food manufacturers make a variety of products on the same production line, without sterilizing the equipment in between batches. For example, a company may produce semi-sweet chocolate chips on the same machinery as milk chocolate chips, with the result being the semi-sweet chips may contain traces of milk. Often the only way to find out about such situations (short of eating the food in question and having a reaction to it) is to contact the food manufacturer directly.

Foods can also become "contaminated" with off-limits ingredients while they are in your kitchen. If, for example, someone were to place a knife that has peanut butter on it into a jar of jelly, that jelly would now contain peanut, and should not be consumed by a person who has peanut allergy.

My "ingredient-listing protocol"
Throughout this book, I have placed all packaged ingredients that are not "pure" products (such as canola oil) in **bold** as a reminder for you to double-check the ingredient panels of these products. In cases where I know that some varieties of that item commonly contain dairy, egg, or nut ingredients, I have specified "dairy-free" or "egg-free" or whatever.

For example, because most margarines contain milk or milk derivatives, all recipes in this book that require margarine specify "dairy-free **margarine**." This does not mean that you should not also check the ingredient panel of your margarine for eggs and nuts. This means that, as of the time of this writing, I personally have never seen eggs or nuts listed as ingredients in margarine – although I have seen dairy products listed as margarine ingredients.

Remember, it is always your responsibility to ensure that every ingredient you use is completely dairy-, egg- and nut-free.

Speaking of margarine...
While we're on the subject of margarine, a good margarine can make a big difference in many recipes, especially in baked goods. Try to find a dairy-free margarine with a low water content and a good taste. You may have to do some searching and taste-testing for the best dairy-free margarine sold in your area.

And now, (drum roll, please): The List
The following is a listing of many of the ways in which milk products, milk derivatives, eggs, and nuts may be listed on an ingredient panel.

This listing is not intended as a substitute for medical advice; always consult with your physician regarding your specific dietary needs and limitations.

Milk Products (also known as "Dairy Products")
casein (this is milk protein)

sodium caseinate or any other sort of caseinate

lactose

lactalbumen

lactoglobulin

whey

curds

milk, milk solids, buttermilk, dry milk, goat's milk

butter, butterfat

cheese

most brands and varieties of soy cheese
(most contain casein)

cream, half and half, whipped cream, whipping cream,
sour cream

Cool Whip® and most other brands of "Non-Dairy Whipped
Topping" (contain casein)

yogurt, frozen yogurt

ice cream, ice milk, sherbet

milk chocolate

pudding

Recaldent (a dairy-derived ingredient found in some chewing
gums)

anything that is labeled "Kosher Dairy" — look on the front of
the product label for a small K or a U, followed by a small
D or followed by the word "Dairy". If there are no dairy
ingredients listed in the ingredient panel, the "Kosher
Dairy" label indicates that the product is made on
equipment that may be "contaminated" with dairy
ingredients, and therefore may not be safe for a milk-
allergic individual to consume.

"Simplesse®" artificial fat (this is made from skim milk and
egg whites)

Eggs

albumin (this is egg protein)

eggs, egg whites, egg yolks, egg shells, egg solids

liquid egg substitute (such as "Egg Beaters®")

livetin

globulin

anything with the word "ovo" in it

"Simplesse®" artificial fat (this is made from skim milk and
egg whites)

Nuts and Peanuts*

peanuts

peanut oil

all tree nuts, including (but not limited to) almonds,
beechnuts, Brazil nuts, cashews, chestnuts, filberts,
hazelnuts, macadamia nuts, pistachios, and walnuts

all nut oils (such as walnut oil and almond oil)

all nut pastes (such as almond paste, used in some baked
goods and in marzipan)

* Technically, peanuts are legumes and are not true "nuts."
Peanuts are one of the most allergenic of the common food
allergens, and are responsible for the majority of food
allergy-related deaths in the United States. All recipes in
this book are completely free of both peanuts and tree nuts.

Basic Recipe Information

General Information

Preparation times are approximate, and assume that all ingredients and equipment needed have been assembled prior to beginning the recipe preparation.

Cooking times are approximate, due to variations in ovens, oven temperatures, and altitude.

Preheating oven: Always preheat your oven to the specified temperature before placing the dish in the oven. Although heating times will vary, most ovens will heat to the designated temperature in about ten minutes.

How to Measure Ingredients

Liquid ingredients: Place liquid measuring cup on level surface, pour in ingredient, and read markings on cup at eye level.

Brown sugar: Using the back of a spoon, pack brown sugar firmly into appropriate-sized dry measuring cup until even with the rim of the measuring cup. When inverted out of the measuring cup, brown sugar should hold its shape.

Dry ingredients: Spoon ingredient loosely into appropriate-sized dry measuring cup or measuring spoon, piling high; level off with a metal spatula or straight-sided knife.

Solid Shortening: Using a rubber spatula, pack shortening into appropriate-sized dry measuring cup. Run spatula through shortening to release air; pack again and level off.

Standard Baking Ingredients

Egg substitute: I have used a combination of vegetable oil, water, and baking powder as an egg substitute in baked goods. These ingredients must be mixed together in a separate bowl or cup until the mixture "fizzes" and the baking powder dissolves, and then added to the recipe as directed. For best results you should complete the recipe immediately after mixing the oil-water-baking powder mixture; do not set the unfinished batter aside to complete it later in the day.

Margarine is dairy-free margarine, and is not "whipped" margarine. Try to find one with a low water content and a "buttery" taste. A good margarine can make a big difference in many of these recipes; if you are not satisfied with the performance of your margarine, try to find another acceptable brand.

Flour is all-purpose flour, unless whole wheat flour is specified.

Sugar is 100% pure cane granulated sugar unless brown sugar or powdered sugar is specified.

Brown sugar: the recipes were all tested using 100% pure cane dark brown sugar.

Powdered sugar is also known as "confectioner's sugar."

Vegetable oil is 100% soybean oil. In all baked goods recipes in this book, canola oil can be substituted for vegetable oil as desired.

Shortening is 100% vegetable shortening; do not use the "butter-flavored" varieties, as these may contain milk.

White distilled vinegar is sold in bottles labeled as such, and should not be confused with white wine vinegar.

Cocoa is 100% pure cocoa powder.

Chocolate chips are dairy-free semi-sweet chocolate chips. Please note that most semi-sweet chocolate chips available in the supermarket are made on the same production line as milk chocolate chips, and therefore may not be safe for those with severe food allergies. In this case, look for "completely dairy-free" chocolate chips at Natural Foods and specialty stores.

Notes

Soups & Salads

Best Ever
Chicken and Orange Salad

I prefer to make this refreshing main-dish salad using boiled chicken, but it will work well with whatever leftover chicken you happen to have on hand.

Preparation time: 10 to 15 minutes

- 1/2 medium-size head of iceberg lettuce, chilled
- 2 navel oranges, chilled
- 1 cup cooked & shredded **chicken** (remove skins before shredding), chilled
- 1 cup **chow mien noodles** (available in the "oriental" section of the supermarket)
- 1/2 cup thinly sliced celery
- 4-1/2 tablespoons **raspberry vinegar**
- 3 tablespoons canola oil
- 1 tablespoon poppy seeds

Shred lettuce into bite-size pieces; place in large salad bowl. Peel oranges, divide into sections, and chop into approximately 1/2-inch pieces. Place chopped oranges on top of lettuce. Add shredded chicken, chow mien noodles, and celery to salad.

To make dressing, mix together raspberry vinegar, canola oil, and poppy seeds. Pour dressing over salad. Toss salad and serve immediately.

Makes 4 servings

Be sure each ingredient used is completely milk-, egg-, and nut-free (see pages 13-15)

Creamy Sweet Potato Soup

This soup has a wonderful, creamy consistency.
It's perfect as a luncheon or supper soup,
but I find it a bit too filling to be used as a first course soup.

Preparation time: 10 minutes
Cooking time: 25 minutes

1 pound sweet potatoes
1 (14-1/2 ounce) can dairy-free fat-free reduced sodium
chicken broth
1/8 teaspoon ground cinnamon
1/8 teaspoon ground nutmeg

Peel the sweet potatoes and cut into 1-inch chunks. Place the prepared potatoes and the chicken broth in a 2 quart pot; cover and bring to a boil over high heat. Reduce heat to low and simmer, covered, 20 minutes or until potatoes are soft.

Using a slotted spoon, remove sweet potatoes from the pot and place in workbowl of a food processor which has been fitted with the metal blade. Add about 1/4 cup of the broth; process until pureed. Pour pureed sweet potatoes back into the chicken broth in the pot; add cinnamon and nutmeg. Stir until smooth. Serve hot.

Makes 2 servings (approximately 1 cup each)

Be sure each ingredient used is completely milk-, egg-, and nut-free
(see pages 13-15)

Dilled Cucumber and Bay Shrimp Salad

*This makes a light, "summery" salad
that is perfect for a side dish or a luncheon first course.*

Preparation time: 13 minutes

Salad:

1 medium cucumber, chilled
1/4 cup minced celery
1 tablespoon minced red bell pepper
1/2 pound cold cooked bay shrimp, washed and drained

Dressing:

2 tablespoons rice vinegar
2 tablespoons canola oil
1 teaspoon **Dijon mustard**
1 teaspoon dried dill weed
1/2 teaspoon bottled minced **garlic**
salt and pepper, to taste

Peel cucumber; cut cucumber in half lengthwise and then slice thinly. Mince celery and bell pepper. Place cucumber, celery, red bell pepper, and shrimp in serving bowl.

Place dressing ingredients in small mixing bowl; mix well. Pour dressing over salad; toss gently to coat. Serve.

Makes 6 servings (about 1/2 cup each)

*Be sure each ingredient used is completely milk-, egg-, and nut-free
(see pages 13-15)*

Fast & Easy
Spinach and Tuna Salad

With this recipe, a healthy lunch is ready in minutes.

Preparation time: 5 minutes

1 (6.5 ounce) can dairy-free **chunk light tuna** packed in
water, drained

1 (6 ounce) package pre-washed fresh baby spinach

1 (8-3/4 ounce) can whole kernel **corn** with no salt added,
drained

2 green onions, chopped (include green tops)

1/2 cup dairy-free bottled **Italian Dressing**

Flake tuna with a fork to break up into small pieces. Place
spinach, tuna, corn and green onions in a large salad bowl.
Toss salad with dressing; serve.

Makes 2 main-course servings

*Be sure each ingredient used is completely milk-, egg-, and nut-free
(see pages 13-15)*

Fat-Free Creamy Carrot Soup

The fresh carrot flavor of this surprisingly rich and creamy soup is complimented by just a hint of nutmeg.

Preparation time: 6 to 8 minutes
Cooking time: 45 minutes

1 (14.5 ounce) can dairy-free fat-free reduced sodium **chicken broth**

6 medium carrots, peeled and cut into 1-inch long pieces (about 2-1/2 cups cut carrots)

1 medium white rose potato, peeled and cut into eighths

1/8 teaspoon ground nutmeg

Place broth and prepared vegetables in 3-quart pot; cover and bring to a boil over high heat. Reduce heat to low and simmer, covered, for 40 minutes, until vegetables are very soft.

Using a slotted spoon, remove vegetables from pot and place in workbowl of a food processor that has been fitted with the metal blade. Process until completely smooth. Return vegetable puree to pot, add nutmeg, and stir until completely blended. Serve hot.

Makes 2 servings (1 cup each)

Be sure each ingredient used is completely milk-, egg-, and nut-free (see pages 13-15)

Fruited Carrot Salad

This salad, which is one of my son Kevin's favorites,
is great to serve at a luncheon buffet, picnic, or barbecue.

Preparation Time: 10 minutes
Marinating Time: 4 hours

1 (1 pound) bag pre-peeled carrots

2/3 cup mixed dried fruit bits (buy the variety that contains
  raisins, apples, apricots and peaches)

3 tablespoons **raspberry vinegar**

3 tablespoons canola oil

2 tablespoons olive oil

1/2 teaspoon ground cinnamon

Freshly ground black pepper, to taste

Using the shredding disk of a food processor, grate the carrots.
Place carrots in serving bowl; add dried fruit bits and mix
well. In a small bowl, combine remaining ingredients to make
dressing. Pour dressing over salad; toss well to coat.
Refrigerate for at least 4 hours. Serve cold.

Makes 8 servings

Be sure each ingredient used is completely milk-, egg-, and nut-free
(see pages 13-15)

Hearty Potato Salad

This makes a rustic, hearty lunch salad.
Serve with a green salad or a fresh fruit salad.

Preparation time: 15 minutes
Cooking time 13 minutes
Refrigeration time: at least 3 hours

1-3/4 pounds red new potatoes, cut into 3/4-inch chunks

3/4 cup (approximately 4 ounces) **Kosher salami**, cut into 1/4-inch cubes

one 4-inch long **Kosher pickle**, diced

3 tablespoons olive oil

2 tablespoons white wine vinegar

1 tablespoon **Dijon mustard**

1 teaspoon sugar

1/2 teaspoon crumbled dried oregano leaves

freshly ground black pepper, to taste

Place prepared potatoes in a 4 quart pot and add enough water to barely cover the potatoes. Cover pot and bring to a boil over high heat. Reduce heat to low and simmer, covered, for 13 minutes or until potatoes feel tender when pierced with a fork. Drain.

To make dressing, place olive oil, white wine vinegar, Dijon mustard, sugar, oregano, and black pepper in a small bowl; mix well.

Place cooked, drained potatoes, prepared salami and pickles, and dressing in a large serving bowl; toss gently. Cover and refrigerate for at least 4 hours, until thoroughly chilled. Serve cold.

Makes 4 servings (a little over 1 cup each)

Be sure each ingredient used is completely milk-, egg-, and nut-free
(see pages 13-15)

Linda's Corn Salad

This quick and attractive corn salad is a great accompaniment dish for chicken or beef, and can easily be multiplied for barbecues and potlucks. One of my friends even likes to use it as a salsa, with tortilla chips.

Preparation time: 5 minutes

1 chilled (11-ounce) can whole kernel corn, drained

3 tablespoons room temperature julienne sliced **sun-dried tomatoes** in oil, drained

1/2 tablespoon oil from sun-dried tomatoes

2 tablespoons minced green onions, green tops only

1 tablespoon balsamic vinegar

1 teaspoon bottled minced **garlic**

1 teaspoon crumbled dried oregano leaves

freshly ground black pepper, to taste

Place all ingredients in serving bowl; mix well. Serve.

Makes 4 servings (1/2 cup each)

Be sure each ingredient used is completely milk-, egg-, and nut-free
(see pages 13-15)

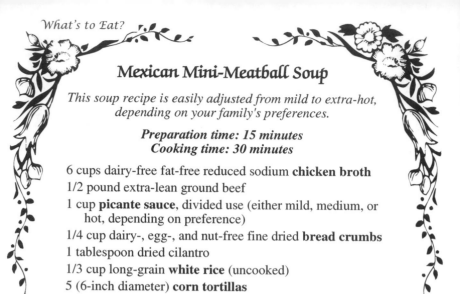

Mexican Mini-Meatball Soup

*This soup recipe is easily adjusted from mild to extra-hot,
depending on your family's preferences.*

Preparation time: 15 minutes
Cooking time: 30 minutes

6 cups dairy-free fat-free reduced sodium **chicken broth**

1/2 pound extra-lean ground beef

1 cup **picante sauce**, divided use (either mild, medium, or
    hot, depending on preference)

1/4 cup dairy-, egg-, and nut-free fine dried **bread crumbs**

1 tablespoon dried cilantro

1/3 cup long-grain **white rice** (uncooked)

5 (6-inch diameter) **corn tortillas**

1 teaspoon **vegetable oil**

1 (8.5 ounces) can unsalted whole kernel **corn**, drained

1/4 teaspoon chile powder (or more, to taste)

Place chicken broth in 4-quart pot. Cover and bring to a boil
over high heat.

While broth is boiling, prepare meatballs. Mix together the
ground beef, 1/4 cup picante sauce, bread crumbs and cilantro.
Form into 1/2-inch-diameter balls.

When broth has boiled, add rice and meatballs. Reduce heat
to simmer, cover, and cook for 25 minutes, stirring
occasionally.

While soup cooks, prepare tortilla strips. Preheat oven to 375
degrees F. Cut tortillas into narrow strips, and then cut strips
in half crosswise. Toss tortilla strips with vegetable oil on a
jelly-roll pan until coated. Spread out into a single layer.
Bake, stirring once after first 5 minutes of cooking time, until
lightly toasted and crisp, about 10 minutes total. When done,
set aside.

When soup has cooked for 25 minutes, add corn, chile
powder, and remaining 3/4 cup picante sauce to soup.
Ladle hot soup into bowls; top with cooked tortilla strips.
Serve immediately.

Makes 6 servings

*Be sure each ingredient used is completely milk-, egg-, and nut-free
(see pages 13-15)*

New Potato Salad

This is a wonderful potato salad for picnics and potlucks; because it doesn't contain any mayonnaise it won't spoil the moment you get it out into the sun! This sure-to-please recipe can also be doubled or tripled for a crowd.

Preparation time: 15 minutes
Cooking time: 35 minutes

2 pounds red-skinned new potatoes
4 green onions, trimmed and cut into thin slices
3 tablespoons **apple cider vinegar**
½ cup olive oil
1 teaspoon **Dijon mustard**
garlic salt, to taste
freshly ground black pepper, to taste

Place potatoes in 4-quart pot and cover with water by about 1/2 inch; add a pinch of salt to water in pot. Bring to a boil, then cover and reduce heat to simmer. Simmer for about 25 minutes or until a knife easily pierces the center of the largest potato. Drain in colander.

When potatoes have cooled slightly, cut into approximately ¾-inch chunks (if you used tiny potatoes you may not need to cut them). Put cut potatoes in large serving bowl. Add green onions.

To prepare vinaigrette, stir together apple cider vinegar, olive oil, Dijon, garlic salt, and pepper until well blended. Pour vinaigrette over potato mixture and gently toss to coat. Serve either at room temperature or cold. Can be prepared one day ahead of serving.

Makes 8 servings (3/4 cup each)

Be sure each ingredient used is completely milk-, egg-, and nut-free
(see pages 13-15)

Onion Soup

This makes a good, basic onion soup

Preparation time: 15 to 20 minutes
Cooking time: 15 minutes

1 medium red onion
1 medium white onion
1 tablespoon olive oil
1 (14-1/2 ounces) can dairy-free 99% Fat-Free **Beef Broth**
¼ cup sherry
½ teaspoon paprika
freshly ground black pepper, to taste

Slice onions into thin slices. Cut each slice in half and then break up into half-rings. Heat olive oil in a 3-quart pot over medium-high heat. Sauté onions until soft and translucent, stirring frequently, approximately 6 minutes. Stir in remaining ingredients. Cover and bring to a boil over high heat. Reduce heat to low and simmer, covered, for 15 minutes. Serve hot.

Makes 3 servings (1 cup each)

Be sure each ingredient used is completely milk-, egg-, and nut-free (see pages 13-15)

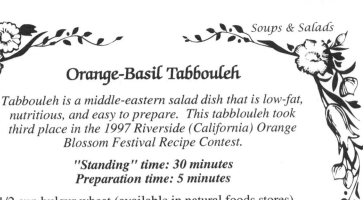

Orange-Basil Tabbouleh

Tabbouleh is a middle-eastern salad dish that is low-fat, nutritious, and easy to prepare. This tabblouleh took third place in the 1997 Riverside (California) Orange Blossom Festival Recipe Contest.

"Standing" time: 30 minutes
Preparation time: 5 minutes

1/2 cup bulgur wheat (available in natural foods stores)
1-1/2 cups boiling water
1 navel orange, peeled, sectioned, and chopped
2 tablespoons chopped fresh sweet basil leaves
1 chopped green onion, including green top
1-1/2 tablespoons orange juice
1-1/2 tablespoons vegetable oil
1/4 teaspoon **lemon pepper**
optional: salt to taste

Place bulgur wheat in medium bowl and cover with boiling water. Let stand 30 minutes; drain.

Place drained bulgur wheat in serving bowl. Add rest of ingredients; toss well. Serve chilled or at room temperature.

Makes 4 servings

Be sure each ingredient used is completely milk-, egg-, and nut-free (see pages 13-15)

Oriental Vinaigrette

Toss this dressing with a fresh green salad.

Preparation time: 5 minutes

1/4 cup canola oil
2 tablespoons lemon juice
2 tablespoons dairy-free **soy sauce**
2 tablespoons rice vinegar
2 teaspoons **Dijon mustard**
1/4 teaspoon peeled and finely minced fresh ginger root
salt and pepper to taste

Place all ingredients in bottle with tightly-fitting lid; shake
well. Serve at room temperature or chilled;
store in refrigerator.

Makes about 2/3 cup vinaigrette

Be sure each ingredient used is completely milk-, egg-, and nut-free
(see pages 13-15)

Tabbouleh Celebration

*This very attractive salad is light and refreshing,
a perfect accompaniment dish for a hot day.*

"Standing" time: 30 minutes
Preparation time: 15 minutes
Refrigeration time: 2 hours

1/2 cup bulgur wheat (available in natural foods stores)
1-1/2 cups boiling water
1/2 cup grated carrot (approximately 1 small carrot)
1/3 cup minced cucumber
1/4 cup minced red bell pepper
2 chopped green onions, including green tops
2 tablespoons chopped fresh oregano
2 tablespoons chopped fresh sweet basil leaves
2 tablespoons fresh thyme leaves
2 tablespoons freshly squeezed lemon juice
1 tablespoon olive oil
1/4 teaspoon salt
freshly ground black pepper, to taste

Place bulgur wheat in medium bowl and cover with the
boiling water; let stand 30 minutes. Drain well, and place in
serving bowl.

Grate the carrot, mince the cucumber, mince the red bell
pepper, and chop the green onions. Prepare the fresh herbs.
Add prepared vegetables and herbs to the bulgur wheat in the
serving bowl and mix well.

To make dressing, place lemon juice, olive oil, salt and pepper
in a small bowl; mix well. Add dressing to salad and mix well.
Cover and refrigerate at least 2 hours. Serve cold.

Makes 6 servings

*Be sure each ingredient used is completely milk-, egg-, and nut-free
(see pages 13-15)*

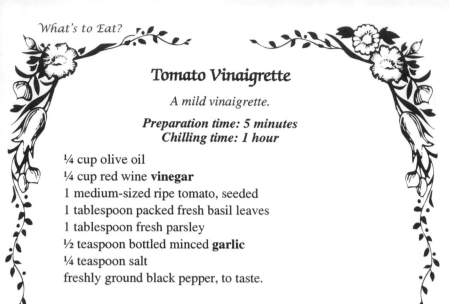

Tomato Vinaigrette

A mild vinaigrette.

Preparation time: 5 minutes
Chilling time: 1 hour

¼ cup olive oil
¼ cup red wine **vinegar**
1 medium-sized ripe tomato, seeded
1 tablespoon packed fresh basil leaves
1 tablespoon fresh parsley
½ teaspoon bottled minced **garlic**
¼ teaspoon salt
freshly ground black pepper, to taste.

Place all ingredients in a blender or in a food processor that has been fitted with the metal blade. Blend or process until completely mixed. Chill at least 1 hour before serving.

Makes 1 cup dressing

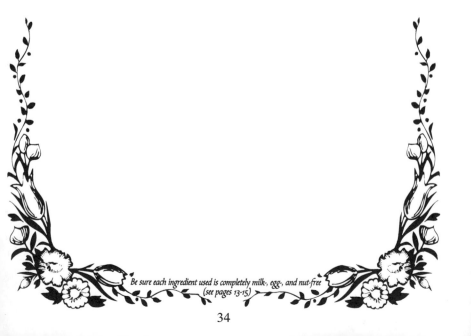

Be sure each ingredient used is completely milk-, egg-, and nut-free
(see pages 13-15)

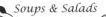

Vegetable-Orzo Soup

This is a satisfying vegetable soup, perfect for a winter supper.

Preparation time: 10 minutes
Cooking time: 15 minutes

2 cans (14-1/2 ounces each) dairy-free fat-free reduced sodium **chicken broth**

1 (14-1/2 ounce) can low-sodium chopped tomatoes, not drained

1 cup chopped fresh broccoli

1 small zucchini, cut in half lengthwise and then sliced thinly

2 large carrots, sliced thinly

1/2 cup uncooked dairy- and egg-free **orzo pasta**

1 teaspoon dried chopped oregano leaves

1 teaspoon dried thyme leaves

1/2 teaspoon garlic powder

1/2 teaspoon onion powder

freshly ground black pepper to taste

Place broth and canned tomato in 3-quart pot; cover and bring to a boil over high heat. While this is boiling, chop the vegetables.

Add vegetables, orzo, and seasoning to boiling ingredients in pot; cover and return to a boil. Reduce heat to low and simmer, covered, for 15 minutes or until vegetables and orzo are tender, stirring occasionally. Serve hot.

Makes 7 servings (approximately 1 cup each)

Be sure each ingredient used is completely milk-, egg-, and nut-free (see pages 13-15)

Notes

Beef

Beef and Vegetable
Skillet Supper

*I like to make this dish with mushrooms, zucchini and onion,
but you can substitute your favorite vegetable combination
in this versatile recipe.*

Preparation and cooking time: 30 minutes

2 cups water
1 cup uncooked **white rice**
1 tablespoon dairy-free **margarine**
1 tablespoon olive oil
8 ounces fresh button mushrooms, sliced
1 small zucchini, cut in half lengthwise and then sliced
1 small onion, chopped
1 (14.5 ounce) can **diced tomatoes**, drained
1 pound extra lean ground beef
1 teaspoon chopped dried parsley
1/2 teaspoon ground thyme
1/2 teaspoon ground sage
1/2 teaspoon garlic powder
freshly ground black pepper, to taste

Place water and margarine in a 2 quart saucepot; cover and
bring to a boil over high heat. Reduce heat to low and stir in
rice. Cook, covered, 15 to 20 minutes or until all water is
absorbed. Remove from heat and set aside.

While the rice is cooking, slice and chop the vegetables.
Heat olive oil in 12-inch skillet over medium-high heat.
Add mushrooms, zucchini and onion and sauté about 6
minutes, until vegetables are soft and reduced in size. Stir
in canned tomatoes. Remove vegetables from skillet and set
in large serving bowl.

Add ground beef to skillet. Brown beef over medium-high
heat until no pink can be seen in the meat, breaking the
ground beef into small pieces as you cook it. Remove from
heat and drain pan drippings from meat.

Add ground beef, cooked rice, and seasonings to
vegetables in serving bowl; mix well. Serve hot.

Makes 6 servings

Be sure each ingredient used is completely milk-, egg-, and nut-free
(see pages 13-15)

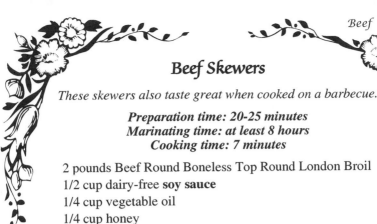

Beef Skewers

These skewers also taste great when cooked on a barbecue.

Preparation time: 20-25 minutes
Marinating time: at least 8 hours
Cooking time: 7 minutes

2 pounds Beef Round Boneless Top Round London Broil
1/2 cup dairy-free **soy sauce**
1/4 cup vegetable oil
1/4 cup honey
1 teaspoon bottled minced **garlic**
1 teaspoon onion powder
1 teaspoon dried ginger powder
1/2 teaspoon black pepper
12 (9-1/2-inch long) wooden or metal skewers

Cut beef into very thin slices. In a medium bowl, combine soy sauce, vegetable oil, honey, garlic, onion powder, ginger, and black pepper; mix well. Add sliced beef to sauce; mix well. Cover and refrigerate for at least 8 hours.

Heat broiler. Line bottom of broiler pan with aluminum foil; spray broiler rack with dairy-free non-stick **cooking spray**. Thread meat onto skewers; place in single layer on prepared pan. Broil for 3 minutes per side, or until cooked through to desired doneness. Serve hot.

Makes 6 to 8 servings

Be sure each ingredient used is completely milk-, egg-, and nut-free
(see pages 13-15)

Flank Steak
with Mustard Sauce

*If you team this up with some microwaved baked potatoes
and fresh steamed vegetables, you can have dinner on the
table in under a half hour.*

Preparation time: 5 minutes
Cooking time: 15 to 20 minutes

1 tablespoon olive oil

1 (1-1/2 pound) flank steak, trimmed of fat

2 teaspoons dairy-, egg-, and nut-free salt-free **seasoning
blend**, such as "Mrs. Dash®," divided use

1/4 cup dairy-free **margarine**

2 tablespoons **Dijon mustard**

Heat olive oil in large frying pan over medium heat. Place
flank steak in pan; sprinkle steak with 1/2 teaspoon seasoning.
Cook, covered, over medium heat for 6 minutes. Turn steak
over and sprinkle other side with 1/2 teaspoon seasoning.
Cook, covered, until flank steak is rare, approximately 5 to 7
minutes. Leaving pan drippings in pan, remove flank steak
and place on cutting board. Let stand for 5 minutes -- flank
steak will continue to cook a little more while standing on the
cutting board. Check doneness of meat; meat should be
medium rare.

To make Mustard Sauce, add margarine, Dijon mustard, and
remaining 1 teaspoon seasoning to pan drippings in pan.
Cook, stirring constantly, over low heat just until margarine
melts. Remove from heat. Stir until sauce is well blended.
Pour into a gravy server.

Slice flank steak, against the grain, into thin strips. Serve with
Mustard Sauce.

Makes 6 servings

*Be sure each ingredient used is completely milk-, egg-, and nut-free
(see pages 13-15)*

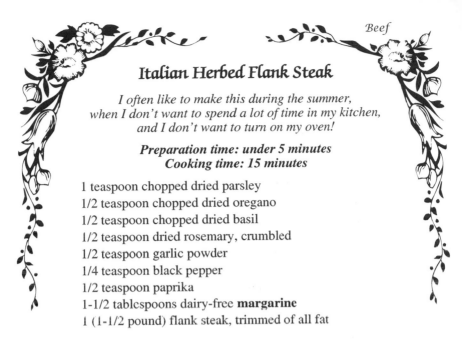

Italian Herbed Flank Steak

*I often like to make this during the summer,
when I don't want to spend a lot of time in my kitchen,
and I don't want to turn on my oven!*

Preparation time: under 5 minutes
Cooking time: 15 minutes

1 teaspoon chopped dried parsley
1/2 teaspoon chopped dried oregano
1/2 teaspoon chopped dried basil
1/2 teaspoon dried rosemary, crumbled
1/2 teaspoon garlic powder
1/4 teaspoon black pepper
1/2 teaspoon paprika
1-1/2 tablespoons dairy-free **margarine**
1 (1-1/2 pound) flank steak, trimmed of all fat

In a small bowl, mix together all ingredients except margarine and flank steak; set aside. Melt margarine in a large frying pan over medium heat. Place flank steak in pan. Sprinkle flank steak with half of the herb mixture. Cook, covered, over medium heat for 6 minutes. Turn steak over and sprinkle with remaining herb mixture. Cook, covered, until flank steak is rare, approximately 5 to 8 minutes.

Place flank steak on cutting board and let stand for 5 minutes - - flank steak will continue to cook a little more while standing on the cutting board. Check doneness of meat; meat should be medium rare. Slice, against the grain, into thin slices. Serve, using the pan juices as a sauce.

Makes 6 servings

*Be sure each ingredient used is completely milk-, egg-, and nut-free
(see pages 13-15)*

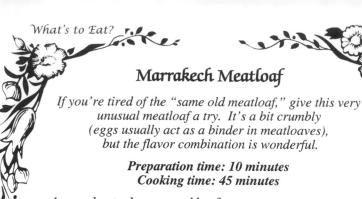

Marrakech Meatloaf

*If you're tired of the "same old meatloaf," give this very
unusual meatloaf a try. It's a bit crumbly
(eggs usually act as a binder in meatloaves),
but the flavor combination is wonderful.*

Preparation time: 10 minutes
Cooking time: 45 minutes

1 pound extra lean ground beef
1/4 cup finely grated zucchini
1/4 cup finely grated onion
1/4 cup finely grated carrots
1/4 cup dried **cranberries**
1/4 cup julienne sliced **sun dried tomatoes** in olive oil
1/2 teaspoon ground cinnamon
1/2 teaspoon ground nutmeg
1/8 teaspoon ground (cayenne) red pepper

Preheat oven to 350 degrees F.

Place all ingredients in a medium mixing bowl; mix well.
Shape mixture into a loaf shape and place in a 7- or 8-inch
square baking dish. Bake, uncovered, in preheated 350 degree
oven for 45 minutes or until done. Serve hot.

Makes 4 servings

*Be sure each ingredient used is completely milk-, egg-, and nut-free
(see pages 13-15)*

Orange Teriyaki Marinated Flank Steak

This marinated flank steak is an absolute favorite of my two boys. It also tastes great when cooked on a barbecue.

Preparation time: 10 minutes
Marinating time: 24 hours
Cooking time: 20 minutes

2/3 cup dairy-free low-sodium **soy sauce**

1/2 cup orange juice

1/3 cup sugar

1/4 teaspoon peeled and finely minced fresh ginger root

2 tablespoons water

1-1/2 tablespoons corn starch

1 (1-1/2 pound) flank steak, trimmed of all fat

To make marinade, place soy sauce, orange juice, sugar, and ginger root in a 1-1/2 quart saucepan. Cover and bring to a boil over high heat, stirring occasionally. In a small bowl or measuring cup, mix water and corn starch; pour into soy sauce mixture. Reduce heat and simmer, uncovered, stirring constantly, for 2 minutes or until marinade thickens. Remove from heat.

Pour half of marinade onto bottom of 9" x 13" glass baking dish. Place flank steak in dish on marinade; pour remaining marinade evenly over top of flank steak. Cover and refrigerate 24 hours, turning steak over once during marinating time.

When you are ready to cook the flank steak, preheat broiler. Line the bottom of a broiler pan with aluminum foil; spray broiler rack with dairy-free non-stick **cooking spray**. Place marinated flank steak on rack of prepared broiler pan. Broil about 7 to 8 minutes on each side, until rare. Place flank steak on cutting board and let stand for 5 minutes --flank steak will continue to cook a little more while standing on the cutting board. Check doneness of meat; meat should be medium rare. Slice, against the grain, into thin strips. Serve hot.

Makes 6 servings

Be sure each ingredient used is completely milk-, egg-, and nut-free (see pages 13-15)

Sautéed Beef with Sun-Dried Tomato Sauce

*Served over dairy- and egg-free **angel-hair pasta** with some fresh steamed vegetables on the side, this is an excellent dish to make for guests.*

Preparation time: 15 minutes
Cooking time: 10 minutes

1/3 cup julienne sliced **sun-dried tomatoes** packed in oil
1/4 cup Balsamic vinegar
1/4 cup olive oil
1 teaspoon **lemon pepper**
1 pound Top Round Beef Round Steak
1 tablespoon olive oil
1 teaspoon **garlic powder**
1/2 cup chopped onion

In a small bowl, stir together sun-dried tomatoes, Balsamic vinegar, 1/4 cup olive oil, and lemon pepper; set aside.

Cut steak into thin strips, and cut each strip into 1 to 1-1/2 inch long pieces.

Heat 1 tablespoon olive oil in 12-inch skillet over medium-high heat. Add steak pieces to pan; sprinkle with garlic powder. Sauté over medium-high heat, stirring often, until meat is cooked (approximately 5 minutes). Remove meat from skillet and set aside. Discard pan juices. Place onion in skillet and sauté over medium heat approximately 2 minutes, until soft. Add cooked meat and sun-dried tomato mixture to onions in skillet. Cook over low heat, stirring constantly, 1 minute or until heated through. Serve over dairy-free **rice** or dairy- and egg-free **angel-hair pasta.**

Makes 4 servings

Be sure each ingredient used is completely milk-, egg-, and nut-free (see pages 13-15)

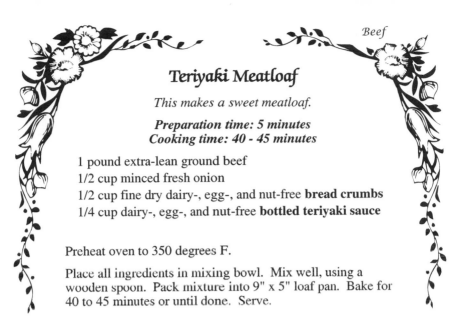

Teriyaki Meatloaf

This makes a sweet meatloaf.

Preparation time: 5 minutes
Cooking time: 40 - 45 minutes

1 pound extra-lean ground beef
1/2 cup minced fresh onion
1/2 cup fine dry dairy-, egg-, and nut-free **bread crumbs**
1/4 cup dairy-, egg-, and nut-free **bottled teriyaki sauce**

Preheat oven to 350 degrees F.

Place all ingredients in mixing bowl. Mix well, using a wooden spoon. Pack mixture into 9" x 5" loaf pan. Bake for 40 to 45 minutes or until done. Serve.

Makes 4 servings

Be sure each ingredient used is completely milk-, egg-, and nut-free
(see pages 13-15)

Notes

Poultry

California Coated Chicken

An easy to make chicken with a tasty coating.

Preparation time: 10 minutes
Cooking time: 25 minutes

2/3 cup apricot or peach **100% fruit spreadable fruit**

2 tablespoons **Dijon mustard**

1/2 cup toasted **wheat germ** (i.e. buy the variety called "toasted")

2 tablespoons **corn meal**

1 teaspoon ground cinnamon

1 teaspoon ground nutmeg

6 boneless, skinless chicken breast halves

Preheat oven to 400 degrees F. Spray a baking sheet with dairy-free non-stick **cooking spray**.

Place apricot or peach spread and Dijon mustard in a microwave-proof shallow dish. Cover and microwave on high for 35 seconds; stir well. Set aside.

Place wheat germ, corn meal, cinnamon and nutmeg in a second shallow dish. Mix well.

Wash chicken; pat dry with paper towels. Dip each piece of chicken in apricot mixture, then dip in wheat germ mixture to coat. Place on prepared baking sheet.

Bake, uncovered, in 400 degree oven for 25 minutes or until done. Serve hot.

Makes 6 servings

Be sure each ingredient used is completely milk-, egg-, and nut-free (see pages 13-15)

Chicken and Rice Luau

*Put on a flower lei and serve this sensational
low-fat dish for a Hawaiian-themed dinner!*

Preparation and cooking time: 30 minutes

3 tablespoons balsamic vinegar

2 tablespoons honey

2 tablespoon dairy-free low-sodium **soy sauce**

2-1/2 cups water

2 large carrots, peeled and sliced thinly into rounds

1-1/4 cup long-grain white **rice**

2 boneless, skinless, chicken breast halves

1 tablespoon canola oil

2 green onions, chopped

1 (20 ounce) can **pineapple chunks** packed in juice, drained

To make sauce, place balsamic vinegar, honey and soy sauce
in a small bowl; mix well. Set aside.

Place water in 2-1/2 or 3-quart pot. Cover and bring to a boil
over high heat. Add prepared carrots and rice; stir. Reduce
heat to low and cook, covered, for 20 minutes or until all
liquid is absorbed by rice. Remove from heat.

While rice and carrots are cooking, prepare chicken. Cut
chicken into 3/4-inch chunks. Heat canola oil in 12-inch skillet
or sauté pan over medium-high heat. Add chicken and 2
tablespoons sauce. Cook, stirring frequently, until chicken is
cooked through. Add chopped green onions; sauté for an
additional 30 seconds. Remove from heat.

Place cooked rice and carrot mixture in serving bowl. Add
cooked chicken and green onion mixture, drained pineapple
chunks, and remaining sauce; mix well. Serve hot.

Makes 4 servings

Be sure each ingredient used is completely milk-, egg-, and nut-free
(see pages 13-15)

Fast and Easy 5-Spice Chicken

This chicken recipe won third place in the Kretschmer Wheat Germ "Healthy Eating Made Easy and Delicious" Recipe Contest.

Preparation time: 7 to 10 minutes
Cooking time: 25 minutes

1/2 cup toasted **wheat germ** (i.e. buy the variety called "toasted")

4 teaspoons **Chinese 5-Spice Seasoning**, divided use

1/3 cup undiluted frozen **orange juice concentrate**, thawed

1 to 1-1/4 pounds boneless skinless chicken breast fillets

Preheat oven to 400 degrees F. Spray baking sheet with dairy-free non-stick **cooking spray**.

In a shallow dish, combine wheat germ with 2 teaspoons Chinese 5-spice Seasoning. In a separate shallow dish, combine thawed orange juice concentrate with remaining 2 teaspoons Chinese 5-spice Seasoning.

Wash chicken breast fillets; pat dry with paper towels. Dip fillets in orange juice concentrate mixture, and then into wheat germ mixture, coating chicken thoroughly. Place on prepared baking sheet. Bake in preheated 400 degree oven for 25 minutes or until cooked. Serve hot.

Makes 4 servings

Be sure each ingredient used is completely milk-, egg-, and nut-free (see pages 13-15)

Golden Coated Chicken Legs

When I first made this chicken, one of my tasters liked it so much that he recommended I name it "Heck-of-a-Good-Chicken."

Preparation time: 15 minutes
Cooking time: 1 hour

8 chicken legs (with skin)

1 (4 ounce) jar **pureed peaches** (i.e. babyfood)

3 tablespoons **Dijon mustard**

1/2 cup toasted **wheat germ** (i.e. buy the variety called "toasted")

1/2 cup **corn meal**

2 teaspoons paprika

1 teaspoon chile powder

1 teaspoon **garlic salt**

1/4 teaspoon black pepper

Preheat oven to 375 degrees F. Spray a 9" x 15" baking dish with dairy-free non-stick **cooking spray**.

Wash chicken legs. Combine pureed peaches and Dijon mustard in a shallow bowl. Place remaining ingredients in a large plastic bag; close bag and shake to mix. Dip first chicken leg into peach-mustard mixture, turning to coat; shake off extra peach mixture. Place this chicken leg in bag with wheat germ mixture. Close bag and shake to coat chicken. Place coated chicken on prepared baking dish. Repeat with remaining chicken legs.

Bake in preheated 375 degree oven for 1 hour or until juices run clear when pierced with a fork. Serve hot.

Makes 8 chicken legs

Be sure each ingredient used is completely milk-, egg-, and nut-free (see pages 13-15)

Italian Style Turkey Meatballs

An easy and healthy entrée.

Preparation time: 10 minutes
Cooking time: 20 minutes

2 (5.5 ounces each) cans 100% **vegetable juice**, room
  temperature
1 teaspoon dried, crumbled oregano leaves
1 teaspoon dried, crumbled basil leaves
1 pound extra lean ground turkey
1/4 cup quick-cooking **oats**

Preheat oven to 350 degrees F. Lightly spray a 9" x 15"
baking pan with dairy-free non-stick **cooking spray**.

Combine vegetable juice, oregano and basil in large
microwavable measuring cup.

In a large mixing bowl combine ground turkey, oats, and
1/4 cup of vegetable juice mixture. Shape meat mixture into
1-inch-diameter meatballs. Place meatballs in single layer,
1/4-inch apart, on prepared pan. Bake at 350 degrees for
about 20 minutes, until cooked through.

Using a slotted spoon or spatula, transfer cooked meatballs to
serving platter. Microwave remaining vegetable juice mixture
for 1-2 minutes on high, until hot; pour over meatballs.
Serve immediately.

Makes 4 - 5 servings

Be sure each ingredient used is completely milk-, egg-, and nut-free
(see pages 13-15)

Lake Forest
Sweet and Savory Chicken

Some people might think that apple butter is a strange ingredient for a chicken dish. I urge you to "throw caution to the wind" and try this dish anyway -- the apple butter forms the base for a thick, sweet and savory (hence the name of the recipe) sauce. Bon Appetit!

Preparation time: 10 minutes
Cooking time: 1 hour

3 pounds cut-up chicken pieces (with bones)

1/2 cup **apple butter** (available in the jam and jelly section of the supermarket)

2 tablespoons **Italian seasoning**

1/2 teaspoon **celery salt**

1/2 teaspoon **garlic salt**

1/2 teaspoon paprika

1/4 teaspoon black pepper

Preheat oven to 350 degrees F. Line a large baking dish with aluminum foil.

Wash chicken pieces and remove skins.

In a small bowl, combine apple butter with seasonings to make sauce. Place chicken in a single layer, bone side up, on prepared baking dish. Using a pastry brush, brush chicken with sauce. Turn chicken over and brush sauce onto other side of chicken pieces. Bake, uncovered, in preheated 350 degree oven for 1 hour, or until juices run clear when chicken is pierced with a fork. Serve hot.

Makes 4 or 5 servings

Be sure each ingredient used is completely milk-, egg-, and nut-free (see pages 13-15)

Mediterranean Chicken

This wonderfully flavorful chicken is one of my favorites to serve to company.

Preparation time: 8 minutes
Marinating time: 7 hours
Cooking time: 35 minutes

4 large boneless skinless chicken breasts halves
1/4 cup julienne sliced **sun dried tomatoes** packed in oil
1/4 cup olive oil
1/4 cup Balsamic vinegar
1 tablespoon grated lemon peel
1 teaspoon bottled minced **garlic**
1/2 teaspoon ground cloves
1/4 teaspoon black pepper
1/2 teaspoon salt (optional)

Wash chicken and place in single layer in baking dish. To make marinade, place all other ingredients in a small bowl and mix well. Pour marinade over and around chicken in baking dish. Cover baking dish and refrigerate at least 7 hours (can be marinated overnight). Turn chicken over in marinade at least once during marinating time.

When you are ready to bake the chicken, preheat oven to 375 degrees F. Bake, uncovered, with all of the marinade sauce in the baking dish, for 35 minutes or until done. Serve hot.

Makes 4 servings

Be sure each ingredient used is completely milk-, egg-, and nut-free (see pages 13-15)

Orange-Sesame Chicken Stir-Fry

A wonderful combination of flavors.
Be sure that the wok that you will be using has not been
"seasoned" with peanut oil.

Preparation time: 20 minutes
Cooking time: 12 minutes

1/4 cup orange juice
1 tablespoon dairy-free **soy sauce**
1-1/2 teaspoons sesame oil
2 teaspoons finely grated orange peel
1 teaspoon bottled minced **garlic**
1/2 teaspoon ginger powder
1 tablespoon canola oil
3 carrots, sliced
3 celery ribs, sliced
1/4 pound fresh Chinese snow peas, trimmed and cut into
   1-inch pieces
3 green onions, chopped
2 boneless, skinless chicken breast halves, cut into 3/4-inch
   pieces
1-1/2 tablespoons **toasted sesame seeds** (i.e. buy the variety
   that is already toasted)

To make sauce, mix togeth er orange juice, soy sauce, sesame oil, grated orange peel, garlic, and ginger powder. Set aside.

Slice carrots and celery, chop green onions, prepare snow peas, and cut chicken. Set aside.

Heat oil in wok. Add carrots and 1 tablespoon sauce and stir-fry for 4 minutes. Add celery and an additional 1 tablespoon sauce to wok; stir-fry for an additional 3 minutes. Add Chinese snow peas and an additional 1 tablespoon sauce to wok; stir-fry for another minute. Mix in green onions. Remove vegetables from wok; place in serving bowl. Add chicken and remaining sauce to wok and stir fry for approximately 3 minutes, until chicken is cooked through. Add chicken to vegetables in serving bowl; mix well.

Serve hot, over dairy-free **rice**. Sprinkle each serving with toasted sesame seeds.

Makes 4 servings

Be sure each ingredient used is completely milk-, egg-, and nut-free
(see pages 13-15)

Plum Crazy Chicken

This chicken has a deliciously sweet and crunchy coating that kids love. You can make it with whichever type of chicken parts your family prefers, but don't plan for leftovers -- the coating becomes soggy by the next day.

Preparation time: 15 minutes
Cooking time: 1 hour

1/3 cup **plum jam**
1-1/2 teaspoons vegetable oil
3 teaspoons **apple cider vinegar**
3 cups dry **Corn Flakes** cereal
2-1/2 to 3 pounds cut-up chicken parts (with bones and skin), washed

Preheat oven to 350 degrees F. Line a baking pan with aluminum foil, and spray with dairy-free non-stick **cooking spray**; set aside.

Mix together plum jam, vegetable oil, and vinegar. Place in a shallow dish and set aside.

Place Corn Flakes cereal in a large plastic bag. Seal bag and roll with rolling pin to crush cereal into small crumbs. Set aside.

Dip chicken pieces one at a time into jam mixture to coat (if necessary, spread the jam mixture onto the chicken with the back of a spoon), and then place chicken one at a time in bag with Corn Flake crumbs. Seal bag, and shake bag to coat chicken with crumbs. Place coated chicken on prepared baking pan. Repeat with remaining pieces of chicken.

Bake chicken in preheated 350 degree oven for 1 hour, or until done. Serve hot.

Makes 4 servings

Be sure each ingredient used is completely milk-, egg-, and nut-free (see pages 13-15)

Seasoned Baked Chicken

Seasoned and baked chicken has been a favorite of mine for many years. Here I am presenting you with basic cooking instructions for Seasoned Baked Chicken and a number of different suggestions for seasoning combinations. You just need to decide how much chicken you want to cook, pick a seasoning blend, cook and enjoy!

Preparation time: depends on quantity of chicken to wash
Cooking time: 1 hour

cut-up chicken pieces (with bones and skin)
canola oil
seasonings

Preheat oven to 350 or 375 degrees F. Line shallow baking dish with aluminum foil. Place washed chicken, skin side down, in single layer on prepared baking dish. Using a pastry brush, brush chicken with oil. Sprinkle generously with each seasoning that is in the desired seasoning combination. Turn chicken over and repeat (i.e. brush with oil and sprinkle with seasonings). Bake, uncovered, in preheated oven for about 1 hour or until done.

Seasoning Combination #1

The cloves give this combination an exotic flavor.

ground thyme
ground sage
ground cloves
ground double superfine (dry) mustard

Seasoning Combination #2

This fills the house with a delicious aroma!

ground thyme
ground marjoram
onion powder
garlic powder
paprika

Seasoning Combination #3

I also like to use this combination on my Thanksgiving turkey.

ground thyme
ground marjoram
ground sage
ground mustard
garlic powder
seasoned salt
paprika

Seasoning Combination #4

Here's yet another delicious combination.

ground sage
ground marjoram
ground mustard powder
onion salt
crumbled thyme leaves
paprika
black pepper

Seasoning Combination #5

The rosemary in this combination gives the chicken a rustic flavor.

dried, crumbled rosemary   parsley flakes
lemon pepper   garlic salt

Be sure each ingredient used is completely milk-, egg-, and nut-free
(see pages 13-15)

Simply Sensational
Chicken Sauté

Serve this fast and easy dish over white rice,
with a mixed green salad and crusty bread,
for non-stop compliments at your next dinner party.

Preparation time: 10 minutes
Cooking time: 10 minutes

2 boneless, skinless chicken breast halves
8 ounces fresh button mushrooms
3 green onions
3/4 cup julienne-sliced **sun dried tomatoes** in oil, drained
2-1/2 tablespoons olive oil from tomatoes, divided use
1 tablespoon **Chinese 5-Spice Seasoning**, divided use

Slice chicken breast halves into thin strips, and then cut strips into 1-inch pieces. Set aside.

Slice mushrooms. Chop green onions (including green tops). Set aside.

Heat 1/2 tablespoon oil in 12-inch skillet over medium-high heat. Add chicken and 1/2 tablespoon Chinese 5-Spice Seasoning and sauté for 3 minutes. Add sliced mushrooms, sun-dried tomatoes, and remaining 1/2 tablespoon Chinese 5-Spice Seasoning and sauté for an additional 3 minutes. Mix in green onions and remaining oil and cook just until heated through (approximately 30 seconds).
Serve immediately, over white rice.

Makes 4 servings

Be sure each ingredient used is completely milk-, egg-, and nut-free
(see pages 13-15)

Sweet and Sour
Turkey Meatloaf

This has become my mother's favorite meatloaf.

Preparation time: 5 minutes
Cooking time: 50 minutes

1/4 cup **apricot jam**
1/4 cup **bottled chile sauce**
1/2 teaspoon bottled minced **garlic**
1/2 cup dairy-, egg-, and nut-free fine dry **breadcrumbs**
1 tablespoon dehydrated onion flakes
1 pound extra lean ground turkey

Preheat oven to 350 degrees F. Lightly grease an 8" x 8" baking dish with vegetable oil, or spray the dish with dairy-free non-stick **cooking spray**.

Place apricot jam, chile sauce, and minced garlic in a large bowl; mix well. Stir in breadcrumbs and onion. Add ground turkey; mix until well blended. Shape turkey mixture into a loaf shape, and place in prepared baking dish. Bake, uncovered, in preheated 350 degree oven for 50 minutes.

Makes 4 servings

Be sure each ingredient used is completely milk-, egg-, and nut-free (see pages 13-15)

Tantalizing Turkey Wraps

*Here's a great way to use up some of your leftover
Thanksgiving turkey -- and it tastes great with
cooked chicken, too!*

Preparation time: 10 minutes

¼ cup bottled **chile sauce**
¼ cup canola oil
1-1/2 tablespoons **raspberry vinegar**
2 cups shredded cooked **turkey**
1-1/3 cup finely chopped celery
1 medium apple, peeled, cored, and grated
4 (8-inch diameter) whole wheat **tortillas**, warmed

Place chile sauce, canola oil, and raspberry vinegar in a
medium mixing bowl; mix well. Add turkey, celery, and
apple; toss to coat.

Spoon one-fourth of the turkey mixture down the center of
each tortilla. Fold sides of tortilla to center, overlapping
edges; fold bottom of tortilla under, completely enclosing
filling. Serve.

Makes 4 wraps

*Be sure each ingredient used is completely milk-, egg-, and nut-free
(see pages 13-15)*

Fish

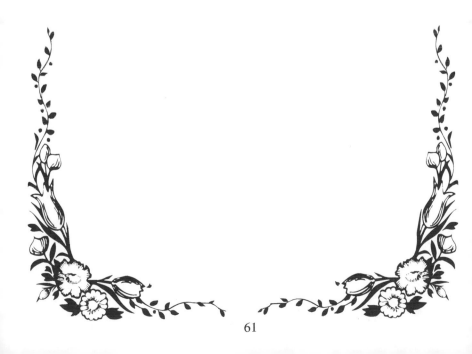

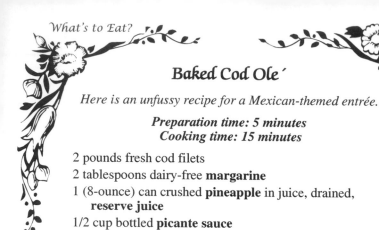

Baked Cod Ole´

Here is an unfussy recipe for a Mexican-themed entrée.

Preparation time: 5 minutes
Cooking time: 15 minutes

2 pounds fresh cod filets
2 tablespoons dairy-free **margarine**
1 (8-ounce) can crushed **pineapple** in juice, drained,
   reserve juice
1/2 cup bottled **picante sauce**

Preheat oven to 375 degrees F.

Place margarine in small microwave-proof bowl; microwave on high for 30 seconds or until melted. Stir in 2 tablespoons of the reserved pineapple juice.

Spray a baking sheet with dairy-free non-stick **cooking spray**. Place cod filets on prepared baking sheet; brush with margarine-pineapple juice mixture. Bake, uncovered, for 7 minutes. Turn fish over, baste with margarine mixture, and bake for an additional 7 minutes or until fish flakes easily with a fork. Remove to serving dish.

To make pineapple salsa, place drained crushed pineapple and picante sauce in a microwave-safe bowl. Microwave on high for 45 seconds; stir. Spoon pineapple salsa over cod in serving dish. Serve immediately.

Makes 6 to 8 servings

Be sure each ingredient used is completely milk-, egg-, and nut-free
(see pages 13-15)

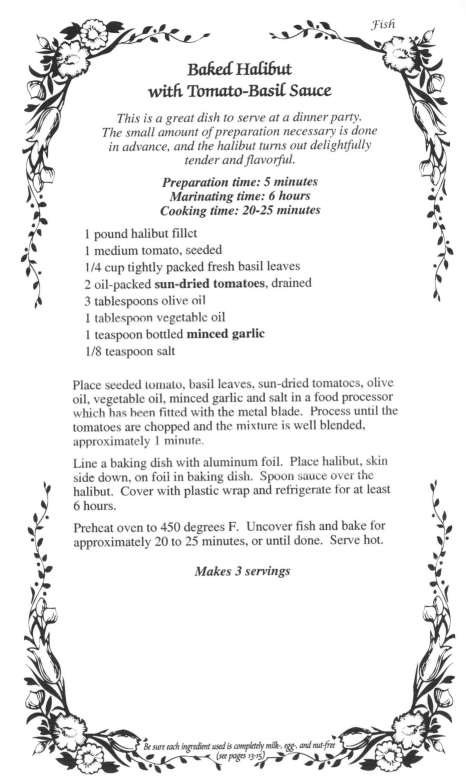

Baked Halibut
with Tomato-Basil Sauce

*This is a great dish to serve at a dinner party.
The small amount of preparation necessary is done
in advance, and the halibut turns out delightfully
tender and flavorful.*

Preparation time: 5 minutes
Marinating time: 6 hours
Cooking time: 20-25 minutes

1 pound halibut fillet
1 medium tomato, seeded
1/4 cup tightly packed fresh basil leaves
2 oil-packed **sun-dried tomatoes**, drained
3 tablespoons olive oil
1 tablespoon vegetable oil
1 teaspoon bottled **minced garlic**
1/8 teaspoon salt

Place seeded tomato, basil leaves, sun-dried tomatoes, olive
oil, vegetable oil, minced garlic and salt in a food processor
which has been fitted with the metal blade. Process until the
tomatoes are chopped and the mixture is well blended,
approximately 1 minute.

Line a baking dish with aluminum foil. Place halibut, skin
side down, on foil in baking dish. Spoon sauce over the
halibut. Cover with plastic wrap and refrigerate for at least
6 hours.

Preheat oven to 450 degrees F. Uncover fish and bake for
approximately 20 to 25 minutes, or until done. Serve hot.

Makes 3 servings

*Be sure each ingredient used is completely milk-, egg-, and nut-free
(see pages 13-15)*

Baked Red Snapper
with Fresh Herbs

Cooking the snapper in foil keeps it nice and moist.

Cooking time: 20 minutes
Preparation time: 10 minutes

1 pound red snapper filets
1 tablespoon dairy-free **margarine**, melted
1 tablespoon lemon juice
freshly ground black pepper, to taste
1 green onion, chopped (including green top)
1 tablespoon chopped fresh parsley
1 tablespoon chopped fresh oregano

Preheat oven to 350 degrees F. Place a large piece of aluminum foil in a 9" x 13" baking dish (the foil should drape over the sides).

Place snapper, skin side down, on foil. Drizzle with melted margarine and lemon juice. Sprinkle with pepper. Place chopped green onion, parsley, and oregano on top of fish. Close up foil and fold edges to seal. Bake in preheated 350 degree oven for 20 minutes. Serve hot.

Makes 4 servings

Be sure each ingredient used is completely milk-, egg-, and nut-free (see pages 13-15)

Baked Salmon
with Honey Mustard Sauce

This recipe is easily multiplied or reduced
for any quantity of salmon.

Preparation time: 5 minutes
Cooking time: approx. 20-30 minutes

1/2 cup honey
1/2 tablespoon **Dijon mustard**
1/2 tablespoon fresh squeezed lemon juice
2 tablespoons dairy-free **margarine**
1-1/2 pounds salmon fillet

Preheat oven to 400 degrees F. Cover a large baking dish with aluminum foil.

Place honey, Dijon mustard, lemon juice, and margarine in a small saucepan. Cook, stirring constantly, over medium heat until margarine melts. Set aside.

Place salmon, skin side down, on prepared baking dish. Measure salmon at its thickest part. Baste salmon with sauce. Bake in preheated 400 degree oven, approximately 10 to 15 minutes* for each 1 inch of thickness (for example, if the salmon is 2 inches thick at its thickest point, bake for 20 to 30 minutes). Baste salmon with sauce halfway through the cooking time. Salmon is done when it flakes easily with a fork.

Makes 5 or 6 servings

* Note: I have found that different types of salmon cook differently. For example, "Red Salmon" is much denser, and takes much longer to cook, than "King Salmon." For this reason, it is difficult for me to estimate how long you will need to cook your piece of salmon!

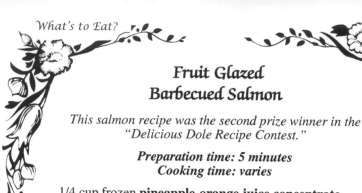

Fruit Glazed
Barbecued Salmon

This salmon recipe was the second prize winner in the "Delicious Dole Recipe Contest."

Preparation time: 5 minutes
Cooking time: varies

1/4 cup frozen **pineapple-orange juice concentrate**, thawed, undiluted

1 tablespoon honey

1 teaspoon dairy-free **margarine**, melted

1 tablespoon grated orange peel

2 pounds salmon fillets

To make glaze, place juice concentrate, honey, melted margarine, and grated orange peel in a small bowl; mix well.

Heat barbecue. Place salmon on barbecue, flesh side down, for 3 minutes. Turn over to skin side down. Brush salmon with glaze several times while it is cooking. Barbecue until fish flakes easily with a fork.

Makes 8 servings

Be sure each ingredient used is completely milk-, egg-, and nut-free (see pages 13-15)

Halibut Stir-Fry

The flavors of this sauce combine well with the halibut.
Be sure to cook this dish in a wok that has not been
"seasoned" with peanut oil.

Preparation time: 12 minutes
Cooking time: 10 minutes

1 pound boneless, skinless halibut fillet
1 (8-ounce) package fresh button mushrooms
1 medium onion
3 tablespoons dairy-free **soy sauce**
2 tablespoons sherry
1 teaspoon sugar
1 teaspoon bottled minced **garlic**
1/2 teaspoon sesame oil
1 tablespoon vegetable oil
1/2 tablespoon cornstarch

Chop halibut into 1-inch chunks; set aside. Slice mushrooms
and chop onion; set aside.

To make sauce, place soy sauce, sherry, sugar, minced garlic,
and sesame oil in a small bowl; mix well.

Heat vegetable oil in a wok. Add halibut and 1 tablespoon
sauce; stir fry 4 to 5 minutes or until cooked through. Using a
slotted spoon, remove cooked halibut from wok. Add
mushrooms, onion, and 2 tablespoons sauce to wok; stir fry 3
minutes or until cooked. Place cooked halibut back into the
wok. Stir cornstarch into remaining sauce and add to wok.
Cook, stirring constantly, until sauce thickens. Serve hot,
over rice.

Makes 4 servings

Be sure each ingredient used is completely milk-, egg-, and nut-free
(see pages 13-15)

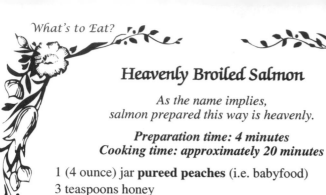

Heavenly Broiled Salmon

As the name implies,
salmon prepared this way is heavenly.

Preparation time: 4 minutes
Cooking time: approximately 20 minutes

1 (4 ounce) jar **pureed peaches** (i.e. babyfood)
3 teaspoons honey
1/4 teaspoon **Dijon mustard**
1/8 teaspoon ground ginger
1-1/2 pounds salmon fillets (approximately 1-inch thick)

Preheat broiler. Line bottom of broiler pan with aluminum foil. Lightly spray rack of broiler pan with dairy-free non-stick **cooking spray**.

To make sauce, place pureed peaches, honey, Dijon mustard and ginger in a small bowl; mix well.

Place salmon fillets, skin side down, on prepared rack of broiler pan. Spread with peach sauce. Broil for 18 to 20 minutes or until done. Serve immediately.

Makes 5 servings

Be sure each ingredient used is completely milk-, egg-, and nut-free
(see pages 13-15)

Pan-Fried Orange Roughy

This delicious fish is quick and easy to make.

Preparation time: about 5 minutes
Cooking time: 10 to 15 minutes

1/3 cup fine dry bread crumbs made from dairy-, egg-, and nut-free **wheat bread**

1 tablespoon minced fresh parsley

1/2 teaspoon **lemon pepper**

1 pound boneless, skinless Orange Roughy fillet

2 tablespoons dairy-free **margarine**

In small bowl mix together bread crumbs, parsley and lemon pepper. Wash but do not dry the Orange Roughy fillet. Place wet fillet on a plate and cover with half of bread crumb mixture. Use your fingers to press the crumb mixture onto the fish. Turn fillet over and cover other side with remaining crumb mixture.

Melt margarine in large skillet over medium heat. Place coated fish in pan and cook for 5 minutes. Carefully turn over and cook for an additional 5 minutes or until done. If the fillet is particularly thick (1 inch or more), cook for 7 to 8 minutes on each side. Serve hot.

Makes 3 or 4 servings

Be sure each ingredient used is completely milk-, egg-, and nut-free (see pages 13-15)

Poached Salmon

This salmon is also delicious served cold the next day.

Preparation time: 2 minutes
Cooking time: 10 to 12 minutes

approximately 1/2 cup sherry
approximately 1/2 cup water
1 pound salmon fillet
1/2 teaspoon dry, chopped dill weed

To help determine appropriate cooking time (see below), measure salmon at its thickest point. Place sherry and water in 12-inch skillet -- you should have about 1/4 inch of liquid in skillet. If there is not enough liquid, add more sherry and water until the liquid level is about 1/4-inch deep. Cover skillet and bring to a boil over high heat. Reduce heat to low and add salmon fillet, skin side down. Sprinkle salmon with dill. Cover skillet and cook over low heat approximately 10 to12 minutes per inch of thickness, until salmon is cooked through. Serve.

Makes 3 servings

Be sure each ingredient used is completely milk-, egg-, and nut-free
(see pages 13-15)

Red Snapper with Savory Rosemary Coating

*The flavors in this recipe combine
to make a very unique dish.*

Preparation time: 7 minutes
Cooking time: 20 minutes

3/4 pound boneless red snapper fillets

2/3 cup toasted **wheat germ** (i.e. buy the variety called "toasted")

1/2 cup orange juice

1 tablespoon dried rosemary, crumbled

1 tablespoon **Dijon mustard**

1 teaspoon bottled minced **garlic**

salt and freshly ground black pepper, to taste

Garnish (optional): fresh rosemary sprigs

Preheat oven to 375 degrees F. Spray a large baking dish with dairy-free non-stick **cooking spray**.

Place red snapper fillets on prepared dish.

In a small bowl, combine wheat germ, orange juice, rosemary, Dijon mustard, garlic, salt and pepper; mix well. Spread wheat germ mixture evenly on top of fish fillets. Bake, uncovered, in 375 degree oven for 20 minutes or until fish flakes easily with fork.

Serve hot, garnished with rosemary sprigs.

Makes 3 servings

*Be sure each ingredient used is completely milk-, egg-, and nut-free
(see pages 13-15)*

Salmon with Tomato and Herb Topping

This is a great recipe for serving to company --
it's elegant, delicious, simple to make, and easily multiplied
for the number of servings you need.

Preparation time: 5 to 8 minutes
Marinating time: 4 hours
Cooking time: 30 minutes

1/3 cup seeded and chopped vine-ripened tomato
1/3 cup julienne sliced **sun-dried tomatoes** in oil
2 tablespoons chopped fresh oregano
2 tablespoons chopped fresh chives
2 tablespoons olive oil
1 teaspoon bottled minced **garlic**
freshly ground black pepper, to taste
1 pound salmon fillet (approximately 1 inch thick)

Place all ingredients except salmon in a mixing bowl; mix
well. Spray a shallow baking dish with dairy-free non-stick
cooking spray. Place salmon, skin side down, on prepared
dish. Spoon tomato mixture over top of salmon. Cover and
refrigerate for at least 4 hours.

Preheat oven to 450 degrees. Bake salmon (with tomato
topping in place), uncovered, for 30 minutes or until done.
Serve hot.

Makes 3 servings

Be sure each ingredient used is completely milk-, egg-, and nut-free
(see pages 13-15)

Pasta

Angel Hair Pasta
with Sesame-Ginger Dressing

*This pasta is equally delicious served hot as a side dish
or cold as a salad.*

Preparation and cooking time: 20 minutes

1 (8 ounce) package dairy- and egg-free **angel hair pasta**
1 small zucchini
1 medium carrot, peeled
<u>Dressing</u>
1-1/2 teaspoons bottled minced **garlic**
1 (1/2" x 1/2" x 1/4") piece of fresh ginger root, peeled
1/4 cup rice vinegar
3 tablespoons canola oil
1 tablespoon sesame oil
salt and freshly ground black pepper to taste

Place approximately 2-1/2 quarts of water in a 4-quart pot.
Cover and bring to a boil over high heat.

While water is boiling, use a food processor that has been
fitted with a shredding disk to shred the zucchini and carrot.
Place shredded vegetables in pot of boiling water. Cook,
uncovered, over medium-low heat for 5 minutes. Add angel
hair pasta to vegetables in pot. Cook, uncovered, over low
heat for 3 to 4 minutes; stir occasionally. Drain.

While pasta cooks, make dressing. Place all dressing
ingredients in a food processor that has been fitted with the
metal blade; process until completely blended.

Place cooked pasta-vegetable mixture in serving bowl.
Add dressing and toss to coat. Serve.

Makes 6 to 8 servings

*Be sure each ingredient used is completely milk-, egg-, and nut-free
(see pages 13-15)*

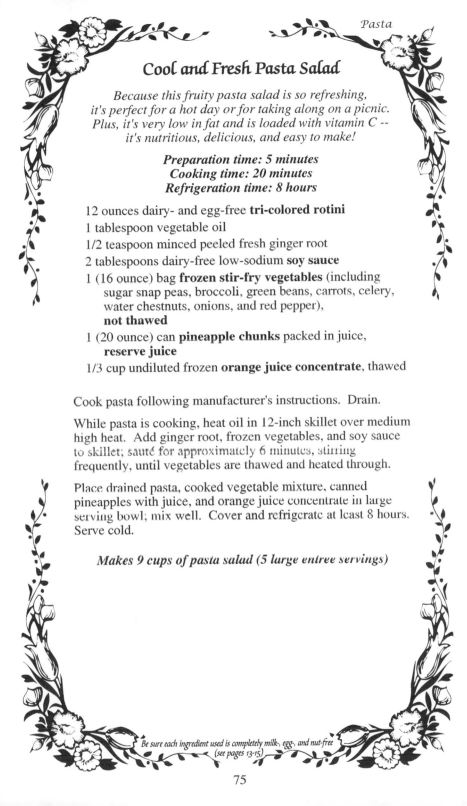

Cool and Fresh Pasta Salad

*Because this fruity pasta salad is so refreshing,
it's perfect for a hot day or for taking along on a picnic.
Plus, it's very low in fat and is loaded with vitamin C --
it's nutritious, delicious, and easy to make!*

Preparation time: 5 minutes
Cooking time: 20 minutes
Refrigeration time: 8 hours

12 ounces dairy- and egg-free **tri-colored rotini**

1 tablespoon vegetable oil

1/2 teaspoon minced peeled fresh ginger root

2 tablespoons dairy-free low-sodium **soy sauce**

1 (16 ounce) bag **frozen stir-fry vegetables** (including
 sugar snap peas, broccoli, green beans, carrots, celery,
 water chestnuts, onions, and red pepper),
 not thawed

1 (20 ounce) can **pineapple chunks** packed in juice,
 reserve juice

1/3 cup undiluted frozen **orange juice concentrate**, thawed

Cook pasta following manufacturer's instructions. Drain.

While pasta is cooking, heat oil in 12-inch skillet over medium
high heat. Add ginger root, frozen vegetables, and soy sauce
to skillet; sauté for approximately 6 minutes, stirring
frequently, until vegetables are thawed and heated through.

Place drained pasta, cooked vegetable mixture, canned
pineapples with juice, and orange juice concentrate in large
serving bowl; mix well. Cover and refrigerate at least 8 hours.
Serve cold.

Makes 9 cups of pasta salad (5 large entree servings)

*Be sure each ingredient used is completely milk-, egg-, and nut-free
(see pages 13-15)*

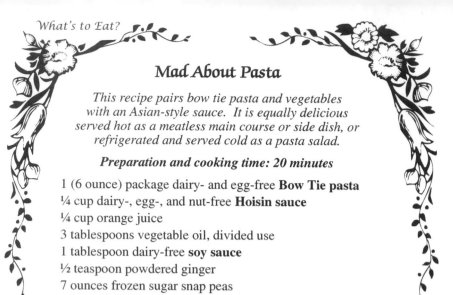

Mad About Pasta

*This recipe pairs bow tie pasta and vegetables
with an Asian-style sauce. It is equally delicious
served hot as a meatless main course or side dish, or
refrigerated and served cold as a pasta salad.*

Preparation and cooking time: 20 minutes

1 (6 ounce) package dairy- and egg-free **Bow Tie pasta**
¼ cup dairy-, egg-, and nut-free **Hoisin sauce**
¼ cup orange juice
3 tablespoons vegetable oil, divided use
1 tablespoon dairy-free **soy sauce**
½ teaspoon powdered ginger
7 ounces frozen sugar snap peas
3 carrots, thinly sliced
2 green onions, chopped

Cook pasta according to manufacturer's instructions; drain.
While pasta is cooking, prepare rest of recipe.

To make sauce, combine Hoisin sauce, orange juice, 2
tablespoons vegetable oil, soy sauce and ginger in small bowl.
Set aside.

Heat remaining 1 tablespoon vegetable oil in 12-inch sauté
pan over medium-high heat.   Add carrots and 1 tablespoon
sauce; cook for 3 minutes, stirring frequently. Add frozen
peas and an additional 1 tablespoon sauce; cook for an
additional 3 minutes, stirring constantly. The peas should now
be thawed and heated through. Add green onions and cook for
additional 30 seconds. Remove vegetable mixture from heat.

Place drained pasta, vegetable mixture and remaining sauce in
serving bowl. Toss gently.

Makes 5 servings (1 cup each)

*Be sure each ingredient used is completely milk-, egg-, and nut-free
(see pages 13-15)*

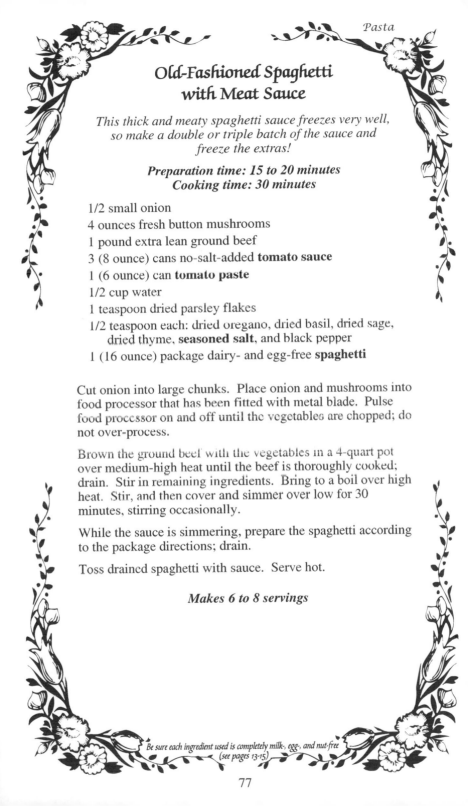

Old-Fashioned Spaghetti with Meat Sauce

This thick and meaty spaghetti sauce freezes very well, so make a double or triple batch of the sauce and freeze the extras!

Preparation time: 15 to 20 minutes
Cooking time: 30 minutes

1/2 small onion

4 ounces fresh button mushrooms

1 pound extra lean ground beef

3 (8 ounce) cans no-salt-added **tomato sauce**

1 (6 ounce) can **tomato paste**

1/2 cup water

1 teaspoon dried parsley flakes

1/2 teaspoon each: dried oregano, dried basil, dried sage, dried thyme, **seasoned salt**, and black pepper

1 (16 ounce) package dairy- and egg-free **spaghetti**

Cut onion into large chunks. Place onion and mushrooms into food processor that has been fitted with metal blade. Pulse food processor on and off until the vegetables are chopped; do not over-process.

Brown the ground beef with the vegetables in a 4-quart pot over medium-high heat until the beef is thoroughly cooked; drain. Stir in remaining ingredients. Bring to a boil over high heat. Stir, and then cover and simmer over low for 30 minutes, stirring occasionally.

While the sauce is simmering, prepare the spaghetti according to the package directions; drain.

Toss drained spaghetti with sauce. Serve hot.

Makes 6 to 8 servings

Be sure each ingredient used is completely milk-, egg-, and nut-free (see pages 13-15)

Pasta Bella

This makes a flavorful meatless main course pasta.

Preparation time: 10 minutes
Cooking time: 10 minutes

1 (12 ounce) package dairy- and egg-free tri-colored
spiral pasta
1 (3 ounce) package **sun-dried tomatoes**
1 medium zucchini
1 (8 ounce) package fresh button mushrooms
1 teaspoon olive oil
1 teaspoon bottled minced **garlic**
freshly ground black pepper, to taste
1-1/2 teaspoons dried basil leaves
3 tablespoons olive oil

Place approximately 3 quarts of water in a 4-quart saucepan.
Cover and bring to a boil over high heat.

While water is boiling, prepare vegetables. Cut sun-dried
tomatoes in half (this is often easiest to do with a kitchen
shears) and set aside. Cut zucchini into quarters lengthwise
and then cut into thin slices. Cut mushrooms into thin slices.

When water has come to a boil, add pasta and prepared sun-
dried tomatoes. Reduce heat to low and cook, uncovered,
stirring occasionally, for 10 minutes or until pasta is al dente.
Drain.

Meanwhile, heat 1 teaspoon olive oil in 10-inch sauté pan.
Add sliced zucchinis and mushrooms, minced garlic, and
black pepper. Cook over high heat, stirring frequently, for 4
to 5 minutes.

Combine cooked pasta mixture, cooked vegetables, basil, and
remaining 3 tablespoons olive oil in large serving bowl.
Mix well. Serve hot.

Makes 6 main-dish servings

Be sure each ingredient used is completely milk-, egg-, and nut-free
(see pages 13-15)

Pasta with
Orange-Tomato Sauce

This pasta sauce is thick and tasty.

Preparation time: 5 minutes
Cooking time: 20 minutes

1 (8 ounce) package dairy- and egg-free **pasta** of your choice

2 (6 ounce) cans no-salt added **tomato paste**

2 cups orange juice

2 teaspoons dehydrated onion flakes

1 teaspoon bottled minced **garlic**

1 teaspoon dried basil leaves

½ teaspoon ground cinnamon

salt and pepper, to taste

Cook pasta according to manufacturer's directions; drain.

While pasta is cooking, make sauce. Place all remaining ingredients in 2 quart saucepot. Cover and bring to a boil over high heat, stirring occasionally until well mixed. Reduce heat to low and simmer, slightly uncovered, stirring occasionally, for 20 minutes.

Toss sauce with cooked, drained pasta. Serve hot.

Makes 4 servings

Rotelle with
Salmon and Mushrooms

This wonderfully satisfying pasta turns a small piece of (often expensive) salmon fillet into dinner for four.

Preparation and cooking time: 25 minutes

1 (8 ounce) package dairy- and egg-free **rotelle pasta**
1 cup sherry, divided use
1 (6 ounce) salmon fillet
1/2 teaspoon dry, chopped dill weed
1/4 cup dairy-free **margarine**
1 (8 ounce) package fresh button mushrooms, thinly sliced
1/2 teaspoon paprika
1/2 teaspoon dried, crumbled oregano leaves
salt and freshly ground black pepper, to taste
2 green onions, chopped (including green tops)

Cook pasta according to package directions. Drain and place in serving bowl.

While pasta is cooking, cook salmon. Place 1/2 cup wine in 8-inch skillet. You should have about 1/4-inch of liquid in the skillet; if you do not, add water until the liquid is about 1/4-inch deep. Cover skillet and bring to a boil over high heat. Lower heat and add salmon fillet, skin side down. Sprinkle salmon with dill. Cover skillet and cook over low heat approximately 12 minutes, until salmon is cooked through. Remove skin and bones from salmon. Using a fork, flake salmon (i.e. break salmon up into small pieces); set aside.

While salmon and pasta are cooking, melt margarine in 10-inch sauté pan over medium-high heat. Add sliced mushrooms, remaining 1/2 cup sherry, paprika, oregano, salt and pepper. Sauté mushrooms over medium-high heat for five minutes.

Combine flaked salmon, sautéed mushrooms with their liquid, chopped green onions and pasta in large serving bowl; gently mix to combine. Serve hot.

Makes 4 servings (approximately 1-1/3 cups each)

Be sure each ingredient used is completely milk-, egg-, and nut-free (see pages 13-15)

Spaghetti with Hidden Vegetable Sauce

I developed this recipe to try to "sneak" some vegetables into my children's mouths. Although it contains no meat, the presence of the minced vegetables in the sauce fools my kids into thinking they're eating spaghetti with meat sauce (which they love), rather than something with vegetables (which, by definition, they think they hate)!

The sauce freezes very well, so feel free to make a double recipe and freeze the extra sauce for another day.

Preparation time: 10 to 12 minutes
Cooking time: 45 minutes

1 medium carrot
1/2 small zucchini
1/2 cup broccoli florets
1/2 small onion
5 fresh button mushrooms
1-1/2 tablespoons olive oil
1 teaspoon bottled minced **garlic**
2 (8 ounce) cans "no salt added" **tomato sauce**
1 (6 ounce) can **tomato paste**
1/4 teaspoon dried oregano
1/4 teaspoon dried basil
1/4 teaspoon dried thyme
1/4 teaspoon dried parsley
1/4 teaspoon salt
1/4 teaspoon black pepper
1 (16 ounce) package dairy- and egg-free **spaghetti**

Using a food processor that has been fitted with a metal blade, mince all vegetables. Heat oil in a 4-quart saucepot over medium heat. Add garlic and minced vegetables and cook, stirring frequently, for 5 minutes. Add all other ingredients except spaghetti and mix well. Partially cover the pot and bring to a boil over high heat. Reduce heat to low, partially cover the pot, and simmer for 45 minutes, stirring occasionally.

During the last 25 minutes of the sauce's cooking time prepare the spaghetti in a separate pot, according to the package directions. Drain spaghetti and toss with sauce. Serve hot.

Makes 8 servings

Be sure each ingredient used is completely milk-, egg-, and nut-free (see pages 13-15)

Spiced Apple Pasta

This sweet pasta is a delicious side dish with poultry or beef, or can be served as a luncheon dish as well.

Preparation time: 5 minutes
Cooking time: 15 to 20 minutes

1 (8 ounce) package dairy- and egg-free **small shells pasta**
2 medium-sized red delicious apples
2 tablespoons dairy-free **margarine**, divided use
1 tablespoon sugar
1/2 teaspoon ground cinnamon
1/2 teaspoon **vanilla extract**

Cook pasta according to manufacturer's directions; drain.

While pasta is cooking, peel, core and dice the apples. Melt 1 tablespoon margarine in small sauté pan over medium heat. Add apples and sauté for approximately 4 minutes, until apples are soft. Add remaining 1 tablespoon margarine and stir until margarine is melted. Remove from heat. Add sugar, cinnamon, and vanilla extract to cooked apples in pan. Toss apple mixture with drained pasta. Serve hot.

Makes 6 to 8 side-dish servings

Be sure each ingredient used is completely milk-, egg-, and nut-free
(see pages 13-15)

Spicy Salmon Pasta

This recipe can be mildly spicy, extra spicy, or somewhere in-between, depending on your choice of taco sauce. If, like my family, your family has a range of tastes, I recommend you cook this up using a mild taco sauce and then pass the hot taco sauce at the table for those who prefer a little fire!

Preparation and cooking time: 25 minutes

1/4 cup bottled **taco sauce**

3/4 cup water

1/2 pound boneless salmon fillet, approximately 1-inch thick

1 (12 ounce) package dairy- and egg-free **spiral pasta**

2 medium-sized ripe tomatoes, chopped

3 green onions, chopped

Dressing:

1/3 cup canola oil

2 tablespoons bottled **taco sauce**

2 tablespoons **white wine vinegar**

1/2 teaspoon chopped dried cilantro leaves

In a measuring cup, mix 1/4 cup taco sauce with 3/4 cup water; pour into 8- or 10-inch skillet. Place salmon fillet in skillet, skin side down. Spoon some of the taco sauce/water mixture over the salmon. Cover skillet and bring to a boil over high heat. Reduce heat to low and simmer, covered, approximately 10 minutes or until salmon is cooked through. Remove cooked salmon from skillet; discard cooking liquid. Remove and discard salmon skin. Using a fork, flake the cooked salmon (i.e. break salmon up into small pieces); set aside.

While salmon is cooking, prepare pasta according to package directions; drain.

While pasta and salmon are both cooking, chop tomatoes and green onions; set aside.

Place dressing ingredients in a small measuring cup or bowl; mix well.

When the pasta and salmon are cooked, place drained pasta, flaked salmon, chopped tomatoes and green onions, and dressing in large serving bowl. Mix well. Serve hot.

Makes 6 servings

Be sure each ingredient used is completely milk-, egg-, and nut-free (see pages 13-15)

Springtime Chicken Rotini

This recipe won an Honorable Mention in the "Exceptional Pastabilities" recipe contest sponsored by the National Pasta Association. My friend Laura's children call it "Chicken Yum-Yum!"

Preparation time: 15 minutes
Cooking time: 15 minutes

3 tablespoons balsamic vinegar
2 tablespoons honey
2 tablespoons dairy-free soy sauce
2 large carrots
1 pound fresh asparagus
2 boneless, skinless chicken breast halves
1 (8 ounce) package dairy- and egg-free tri-color Rotini
1 tablespoon canola oil

To make sauce, mix together balsamic vinegar, honey, and soy sauce; set aside.

Place approximately 2-1/2 quarts of water in a 4 quart pot. Cover pot and bring to a boil over high heat.

While water is boiling, prepare vegetables and chicken. Peel carrots and slice thinly into rounds. Wash asparagus. Remove and discard the rough ends of the asparagus; cut the remaining asparagus into 1-inch long pieces. Cut the chicken into 3/4-inch chunks.

When the water is boiling, place the prepared carrots and asparagus in the boiling water. Cook, uncovered, over medium heat for 5 minutes. Add pasta and cook for an additional 10 minutes over low heat, stirring occasionally.

Meanwhile, heat canola oil in 12-inch skillet or sauté pan over medium-high heat. Add prepared chicken and 1-1/2 tablespoons sauce; sauté until done. Remove from heat.

Drain pasta and vegetables and place in serving bowl. Add cooked chicken and remaining sauce; mix well. Serve hot.

Makes 6 servings

Be sure each ingredient used is completely milk-, egg-, and nut-free (see pages 13-15)

Potatoes

Curried Oven-Baked Potatoes

*These potatoes go well with meat or chicken, for a
"meat and potatoes"-style dinner.*

Preparation time: 10 minutes
Cooking time: 1 hour

2 tablespoons olive oil
2 teaspoons **curry powder**
salt and pepper to taste
2 large Russet potatoes, peeled and diced

Preheat oven to 350 degrees F. Lightly spray a 9" x 13"
baking pan with dairy-free non-stick **cooking spray**.

Combine olive oil, curry powder, salt and pepper in mixing
bowl. Add diced potatoes; toss to coat.

Spread potato mixture in even layer in prepared baking pan.
Bake, uncovered, in preheated 350 degree oven for 1 hour, or
until top is lightly browned and potatoes feel soft when
pierced with a fork. Serve hot.

Makes 4 servings

*Be sure each ingredient used is completely milk-, egg-, and nut-free
(see pages 13-15)*

Easy Winter Potatoes

These hearty potatoes make a perfect side-dish for roast beef or chicken. If you want to double this recipe, simply divide the ingredients into two foil packets. If you over-stuff a packet it will take much longer to cook.

Preparation time: 5 minutes
Cooking time: 1 hour

4 medium red potatoes, cut into bite-size pieces (you should have approximately 4 cups cut-up potato)

½ small onion, cut in half and then sliced

¼ cup olive oil

2 tablespoons **Dijon mustard**

1 teaspoon crumbled dried oregano leaves

½ teaspoon **seasoned salt**

freshly ground black pepper, to taste

Preheat oven to 375 degrees F. Cut a piece of heavy-duty aluminum foil 18 x 24 inches; spray foil with dairy-free non-stick **cooking spray**.

Layer potatoes and onion in middle section of prepared foil. To make sauce, place remaining ingredients in a small measuring cup; mix well. Drizzle sauce over potatoes and onion. Gently stir to coat.

Bring up sides of foil and double fold. Double fold ends to form one large foil packet, leaving room for heat circulation inside packet. Place packet on baking sheet. Bake for one hour. Serve hot.

Makes 4 servings (about 1 cup each)

Be sure each ingredient used is completely milk-, egg-, and nut-free (see pages 13-15)

Glazed Sweet Potatoes with Marshmallow Topping

Sweet, delicious and simple to make.

Preparation time: 8 to 10 minutes
Cooking time: 1 hour

2 medium sweet potatoes
2 tablespoons dairy-free **margarine**
½ teaspoon ground cinnamon
¼ teaspoon ground nutmeg
1 cup dairy- and egg-free **mini-marshmallows**

Preheat oven to 350 degrees F.

Peel sweet potatoes and cut into 1-inch chunks.

Place margarine in microwave-safe measuring cup. Microwave on high for 30 seconds or until melted. Stir in cinnamon and nutmeg.

Place prepared sweet potatoes and margarine mixture in shallow baking dish. Stir to coat, and then spread the potatoes out into a single layer.

Bake in preheated 350 degree oven for 50 minutes. Sprinkle mini-marshmallows over the top of the potatoes; bake for an additional 7 to 10 minutes. Serve hot.

Makes 4 servings

Be sure each ingredient used is completely milk-, egg-, and nut-free (see pages 13-15)

Herbed Oven Roasted Potatoes

This is a great dish to serve with baked chicken.

Preparation time: 10 minutes
Cooking time: 1 hour

2 medium Russet potatoes
2-1/2 tablespoons olive oil
1 tablespoon dried onion flakes
1/2 tablespoon dried rosemary, crumbled
1 teaspoon dried sweet basil leaves
1/2 teaspoon garlic salt
freshly ground black pepper, to taste

Preheat oven to 400 degrees F. Lightly spray a 9" x 13" baking dish with dairy-free non-stick **cooking spray**.

Scrub potatoes, but do not peel. Slice potatoes into very thin slices. Arrange potato slices in a slightly overlapping single layer in the prepared baking dish. In a small bowl or measuring cup, mix together the olive oil, onion flakes, rosemary, basil leaves, garlic salt, and black pepper. Using a pastry brush, brush this olive oil mixture evenly over potatoes. Bake, uncovered, in preheated 400 degree oven for 1 hour or until potatoes are lightly browned and thoroughly cooked. Serve hot.

Makes 4 servings

Be sure each ingredient used is completely milk-, egg-, and nut-free (see pages 13-15)

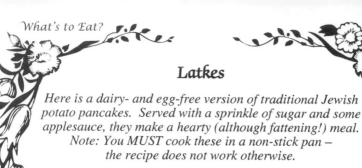

Latkes

Here is a dairy- and egg-free version of traditional Jewish potato pancakes. Served with a sprinkle of sugar and some applesauce, they make a hearty (although fattening!) meal. Note: You MUST cook these in a non-stick pan – the recipe does not work otherwise.

Preparation time: 13 to 15 minutes
Cooking time: 20 minutes

2 medium Russet potatoes, peeled
1/2 small onion
1/2 cup **flour**
1 teaspoon **baking powder**
1/2 teaspoon salt
approximately 1-1/4 cups vegetable oil

Using the grating disk of a food processor, grate the potatoes and the onion. Remove the grated potatoes and onion from food processor work bowl and insert the metal blade into the food processor. Place potatoes and onions back into the food processor; add flour, baking powder, and salt. Process with metal blade until the batter is a well-blended "mush."

Pour enough vegetable oil into a large <u>non-stick</u> frying pan or skillet to make a 1/4-inch layer of oil. Heat oil over medium-high heat for 3 minutes. Drop batter by large spoonfuls into hot oil, forming pancakes that are approximately 2-1/2 to 3 inches in diameter; flatten dough with the back of the spoon. Cook over medium-high heat for 2 to 3 minutes, until edges of latkes turn light brown. Turn latkes over and cook an additional 2 to 3 minutes on the other side, until both sides are browned. Drain cooked latkes on a few layers of paper towels before serving. Repeat with remaining batter. Serve hot, sprinkled with sugar.

Makes about 24 (2-1/2 to 3 inches in diameter)
potato pancakes

Be sure each ingredient used is completely milk-, egg-, and nut-free
(see pages 13-15)

New Potatoes with Sun Dried Tomato Dressing

This potato dish, which is one of my favorites, was a First Prize winner in the national "The Ladies Have Taste" Recipe Contest sponsored by the makers of Mrs. Dash® seasoning.

Preparation time: 10 minutes
Cooking time: 15 minutes

2 pounds tiny new red potatoes, washed

2 green onions

1/4 cup olive oil

1/4 cup balsamic vinegar

1/2 cup julienne sliced **sun-dried tomatoes** packed in oil

1 tablespoon dairy-, egg-, and nut-free salt-free **seasoning blend**, such as "Mrs. Dash®"

Place cut potatoes in 3-quart pot and add enough water to just cover potatoes. Cover pot and bring to a boil over high heat. Turn heat down to low and simmer, covered, for 10 minutes or until a fork can easily pierce the center of the largest potato. Drain potatoes in colander.

While potatoes are cooking, chop green onions (including green tops) and set aside.

To prepare dressing, combine olive oil, balsamic vinegar, sun dried tomatoes and seasoning in a small bowl. Blend well with a fork.

Place drained potatoes and chopped green onions in serving bowl. Pour dressing over potatoes and toss gently to coat. Serve immediately.

Makes 6 side-dish servings

Be sure each ingredient used is completely milk-, egg-, and nut-free (see pages 13-15)

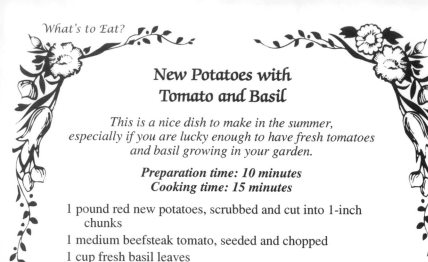

New Potatoes with Tomato and Basil

*This is a nice dish to make in the summer,
especially if you are lucky enough to have fresh tomatoes
and basil growing in your garden.*

Preparation time: 10 minutes
Cooking time: 15 minutes

1 pound red new potatoes, scrubbed and cut into 1-inch
  chunks
1 medium beefsteak tomato, seeded and chopped
1 cup fresh basil leaves
2 tablespoons olive oil
1 teaspoon bottled minced **garlic**
1/2 teaspoon salt
freshly ground black pepper to taste

Place cut potatoes in 2-quart pot and add enough water to just
cover potatoes. Cover pot and bring to a boil over high heat.
Reduce heat to low and simmer, covered, about 12 minutes or
until potatoes are tender when pierced with a fork. Drain.

While potatoes are cooking, seed and chop tomato and set
aside. Place basil, oil, garlic, salt, and pepper in work bowl of
food processor that has been fitted with the metal blade.
Process until basil is chopped, scraping side of work bowl
occasionally.

Place cooked and drained potatoes, chopped tomatoes and
basil mixture in serving bowl. Toss gently to coat.
Serve warm.

Makes 6 servings (3/4 cup each)

Be sure each ingredient used is completely milk-, egg-, and nut-free
(see pages 13-15)

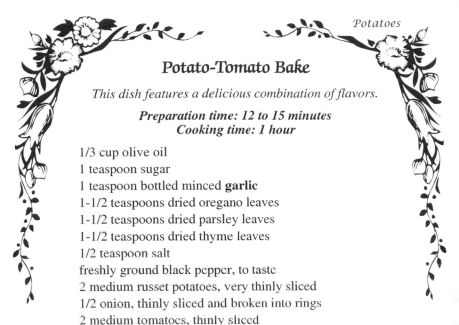

Potato-Tomato Bake

This dish features a delicious combination of flavors.

Preparation time: 12 to 15 minutes
Cooking time: 1 hour

1/3 cup olive oil
1 teaspoon sugar
1 teaspoon bottled minced **garlic**
1-1/2 teaspoons dried oregano leaves
1-1/2 teaspoons dried parsley leaves
1-1/2 teaspoons dried thyme leaves
1/2 teaspoon salt
freshly ground black pepper, to taste
2 medium russet potatoes, very thinly sliced
1/2 onion, thinly sliced and broken into rings
2 medium tomatoes, thinly sliced

Preheat oven to 375 degrees F.

In a small bowl or measuring cup, combine olive oil, sugar, garlic, oregano, parsley, thyme, salt, and pepper.

Arrange sliced potatoes in a single, overlapping layer in a 9" x 13" baking dish. Using a pastry brush, brush potatoes with 1/3 of olive oil mixture. Arrange onion rings in a single layer on top of the potatoes. Brush onions with 1/3 of olive oil mixture. Arrange tomatoes in a single layer on top of the onions. Brush tomatoes with remaining olive oil mixture. Bake, covered, in preheated 375 degree oven for 45 minutes, and then uncovered for an additional 15 minutes. Serve hot.

Makes 6 servings

Simple Sweet Potatoes

*These sweet potatoes make a great side dish
to serve with poultry.*

Preparation time: 5 to 10 minutes
Cooking time: 45 minutes

2 sweet potatoes
¼ cup olive oil
¼ teaspoon paprika
1/8 teaspoon chile powder

Preheat oven to 400 degrees F.

Peel sweet potatoes. Cut potatoes into ½-inch slices, and then
cut each slice into quarters. Arrange sweet potato pieces in a
single layer in 9" x 13" baking dish. Add olive oil, and turn
potatoes to coat them with oil. Bake, uncovered, in preheated
400 degree oven, for 45 minutes or until potatoes are soft but
not falling apart. Sprinkle cooked potatoes with paprika and
chile powder; gently stir potatoes to evenly distribute the
seasonings. Using a slotted spoon, transfer the sweet potatoes
to a serving bowl. Serve hot.

Makes 4 or 5 servings

Be sure each ingredient used is completely milk-, egg-, and nut-free
(see pages 13-15)

Whipped Potatoes

*Although this looks a lot like mashed potatoes,
it tastes much different. The olive oil gives these whipped
potatoes a rich, rustic flavor that I enjoy without any gravy.*

Preparation time: 5 minutes
Cooking time: 25 minutes

1-1/2 pounds white potatoes
3 tablespoons olive oil
1 teaspoon bottled minced **garlic**
1 teaspoon **seasoned salt**
freshly ground black pepper, to taste

Peel potatoes and slice into 1/2-inch thick slices. Place in 3 quart saucepot; add enough water to just cover the potatoes. Cover pot and bring to a boil over high heat. Reduce heat to low and simmer, covered, for 20 minutes or until potatoes feel soft when pierced with a fork. Drain.

Place potatoes back into the pot; add remaining ingredients. Using electric hand-held beaters, beat on high speed until light and fluffy. Serve hot.

Makes 6 servings

*Be sure each ingredient used is completely milk-, egg-, and nut-free
(see pages 13-15)*

95

Notes

Rice

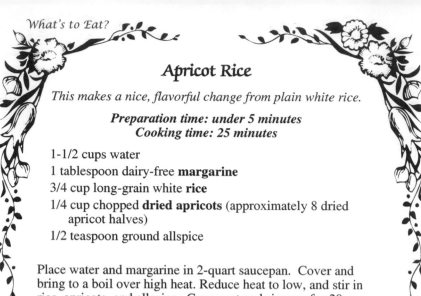

Apricot Rice

This makes a nice, flavorful change from plain white rice.

Preparation time: under 5 minutes
Cooking time: 25 minutes

1-1/2 cups water
1 tablespoon dairy-free **margarine**
3/4 cup long-grain white **rice**
1/4 cup chopped **dried apricots** (approximately 8 dried
   apricot halves)
1/2 teaspoon ground allspice

Place water and margarine in 2-quart saucepan. Cover and
bring to a boil over high heat. Reduce heat to low, and stir in
rice, apricots, and allspice. Cover pot and simmer for 20
minutes or until all water is absorbed. Serve hot.

Makes 4 servings (1/2 cup each)

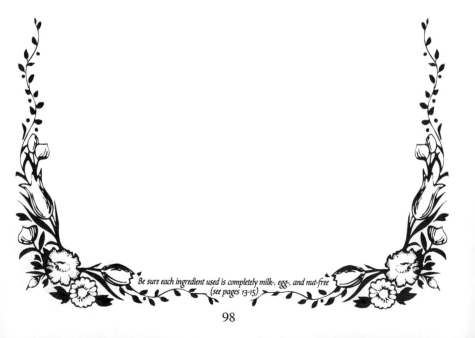

Be sure each ingredient used is completely milk-, egg-, and nut-free
(see pages 13-15)

Basil Rice

*If some members of your family prefer their rice plain,
you can set their serving aside before you add
in the seasonings*

Preparation time: under 5 minutes
Cooking time: 25 minutes

2 cups water
1 tablespoon dairy-free **margarine**
1 cup long-grain white **rice**
1-1/2 teaspoons dried sweet basil leaves, crumbled
3/4 teaspoon **lemon pepper**
¼ to ½ teaspoon **onion salt**, depending on taste

Place water and margarine in 2-1/2 quart saucepot. Cover and
bring to a boil over high heat. Stir in rice, reduce heat to low,
and cook, covered, for 20 minutes or until all water is
absorbed. Stir in basil, lemon pepper, and onion salt.
Serve immediately.

Makes 6 servings (1/2 cup each)

Be sure each ingredient used is completely milk-, egg-, and nut-free
(see pages 13-15)

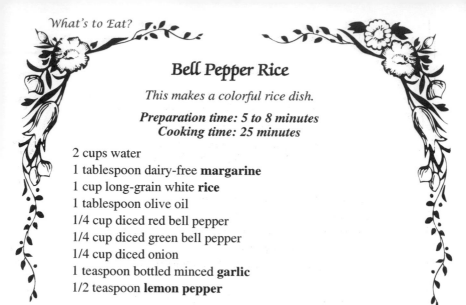

Bell Pepper Rice

This makes a colorful rice dish.

Preparation time: 5 to 8 minutes
Cooking time: 25 minutes

2 cups water
1 tablespoon dairy-free **margarine**
1 cup long-grain white **rice**
1 tablespoon olive oil
1/4 cup diced red bell pepper
1/4 cup diced green bell pepper
1/4 cup diced onion
1 teaspoon bottled minced **garlic**
1/2 teaspoon **lemon pepper**

Place water and margarine in a 2-quart pot. Cover pot and bring to a boil over high heat. Stir in rice, reduce heat to low, and cook, covered, for 20 minutes or until all water is absorbed.

While rice is cooking, heat olive oil in a small frying pan or sauté pan. Add remaining ingredients and cook over medium heat, stirring frequently, for 2 to 3 minutes or until vegetables are soft. Remove from heat. When rice is cooked, combine rice with cooked vegetable mixture. Serve hot.

Makes 6 servings (1/2 cup each)

Be sure each ingredient used is completely milk-, egg-, and nut-free
(see pages 13-15)

Burgundy Wild Rice Pilaf

This rice pilaf goes especially well with turkey or chicken.

Preparation time: 10 to 15 minutes
Cooking time: 50 minutes

2/3 cup Burgundy wine
1 cup water
3/4 cup wild rice, rinsed and drained
1 teaspoon vegetable oil
1/2 cup chopped onion
1/2 cup chopped green or red bell pepper
1/3 cup dried cranberries
1/4 teaspoon salt (or more, if desired)

Place Burgundy wine and water in 3 quart saucepan; bring to a boil over high heat. Add rice. Cover, return to a boil over high heat, and then turn heat down to low. Simmer, covered, for 50 minutes or until rice is tender and liquid is absorbed.

While wild rice is cooking, chop onion and red bell pepper. Heat vegetable oil over medium heat in small sauté pan. Add chopped onions and bell peppers; sauté 3 to 4 minutes or until cooked. Set aside.

Combine cooked rice, cooked vegetables, dried cranberries and salt in serving bowl. Serve hot.

Makes 6 servings (1/2 cup each)

Be sure each ingredient used is completely milk-, egg-, and nut-free
(see pages 13-15)

Heidi's Rice

*My dear friend Heidi Kahn concocted this recipe to serve
at a Halloween party for our food allergy support group.
Everyone just couldn't stop eating it -- one child had three
helpings! I hope this rice is a hit with your family as well.*

Preparation time: 10 minutes
Cooking time: 45 minutes

1 medium onion, chopped
3 tablespoons canola oil, divided use
2 carrots
2 cups water
1 cup long-grain white **rice**
salt and pepper to taste

Chop onion; set aside. Peel carrots and cut into 1/4-inch-thick
slices. Cut each carrot slice into quarters; set aside.

Heat 2 tablespoons canola oil in small saucepan. Add
chopped onions and cook over low heat for 15 minutes,
stirring occasionally. Add carrots and cook over low heat for
an additional 30 minutes, stirring occasionally.

While onions and carrots are cooking, cook the rice. Place the
water and the remaining 1 tablespoon canola oil in a 2 quart
saucepan; cover and bring to a boil over high heat. Reduce
heat to low and stir in rice. Cover pot and cook over low for
20 minutes. Remove from heat and let sit an additional
5 minutes.

Place cooked rice, cooked vegetables, salt and pepper in
serving bowl; mix well. Serve hot.

Makes 6 servings (1/2 cup each)

Be sure each ingredient used is completely milk-, egg-, and nut-free
(see pages 13-15)

Orange-Raisin Rice

This makes a sweet rice dish.

Preparation time: 5 minutes
Cooking time: 20 minutes

2 cups orange juice
1 cup long-grain white **rice**
1 tablespoon honey
1/2 tablespoon canola oil
1/2 tablespoon **raspberry vinegar**
1/2 cup raisins

Place orange juice in 2-1/2 or 3-quart pot; cover and bring to a boil over high heat. Reduce heat to low and stir in rice; cover and cook over low for 20 minutes or until all juice is absorbed.

In a small bowl or measuring cup, stir together honey, canola oil, and raspberry vinegar. Stir this dressing and the raisins into the cooked rice. Serve hot.

Makes 6 servings (approximately 1/2 cup each)

Be sure each ingredient used is completely milk-, egg-, and nut-free (see pages 13-15)

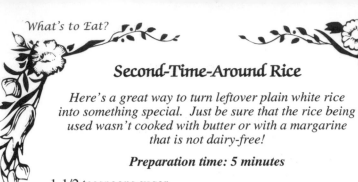

Second-Time-Around Rice

Here's a great way to turn leftover plain white rice into something special. Just be sure that the rice being used wasn't cooked with butter or with a margarine that is not dairy-free!

Preparation time: 5 minutes

1-1/2 teaspoons sugar
1/2 teaspoon dried thyme leaves
1/2 teaspoon allspice
1/4 teaspoon **onion salt**
1/8 teaspoon ground nutmeg
dash of cayenne pepper
3 cups **cooked white rice**, heated

Place sugar, thyme leaves, allspice, onion salt, nutmeg and cayenne pepper in small bowl; mix well. Combine seasonings mixture with heated cooked rice. Serve.

Makes 6 servings (1/2 cup each)

Be sure each ingredient used is completely milk-, egg-, and nut-free (see pages 13-15)

Sun-Dried Tomato Rice

*I love the taste of sun-dried tomatoes, but my kids don't –
so I set their rice servings aside before I add in the
tomatoes and seasonings.*

Preparation time: 5 minutes
Cooking time: 25 minutes

2 cups water

1 tablespoon dairy-free **margarine**

1 cup long grain white **rice**

1/3 cup julienne sliced **sun-dried tomatoes** packed in oil, drained

1 teaspoon bottled minced **garlic**

1/2 teaspoon **lemon pepper**

1/8 teaspoon ground cloves

(optional) salt to taste

Place water and margarine in 2-1/2 or 3-quart pot; cover and bring to a boil over high heat. Reduce heat to low and stir in rice; cover and cook over low for 20 minutes or until all water has been absorbed. Stir in remaining ingredients. Serve hot.

Makes 6 servings (1/2 cup each)

Be sure each ingredient used is completely milk-, egg-, and nut-free (see pages 13-15)

Zucchini and Basil Rice

This makes a great summer side-dish.

Preparation time: 6 minutes
Cooking time: 25 minutes

2 cups water
1 tablespoon dairy-free **margarine**
1 medium zucchini
1 cup long-grain white **rice**
1 teaspoon dried basil, crumbled
salt and freshly ground black pepper to taste

Place water and margarine in 3 quart pot; cover and bring to a boil over high heat.

While water is boiling, finely grate the zucchini using a food processor that has been fitted with a shredding disc (you should have about 1 cup grated zucchini).

When water is boiling add grated zucchini, rice, basil, salt and pepper. Reduce heat to low and simmer, covered, for 20 minutes or until all water has been absorbed. Serve hot.

Makes 7 servings (1/2 cup each)

Be sure each ingredient used is completely milk-, egg-, and nut-free (see pages 13-15)

Vegetables

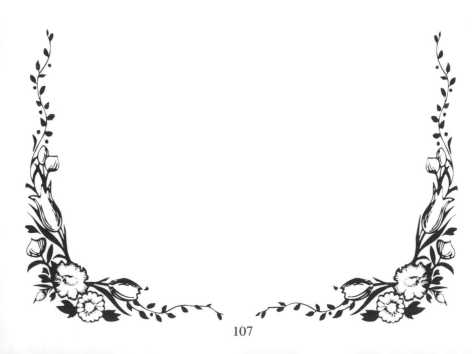

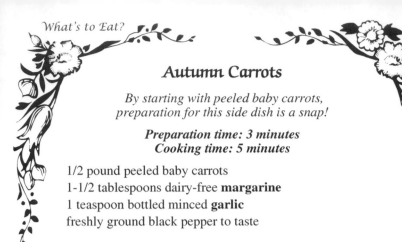

Autumn Carrots

*By starting with peeled baby carrots,
preparation for this side dish is a snap!*

Preparation time: 3 minutes
Cooking time: 5 minutes

1/2 pound peeled baby carrots
1-1/2 tablespoons dairy-free **margarine**
1 teaspoon bottled minced **garlic**
freshly ground black pepper to taste

Using a food processor that has been fitted with the shredding disk, grate the carrots.

Melt margarine in 10-inch sauté pan over medium-high heat. Stir in garlic. Add carrots and black pepper and sauté for approximately 4 minutes, stirring frequently, until carrots are cooked. Serve hot.

Makes 3 servings (1/2 cup each)

*Be sure each ingredient used is completely milk-, egg-, and nut-free
(see pages 13-15)*

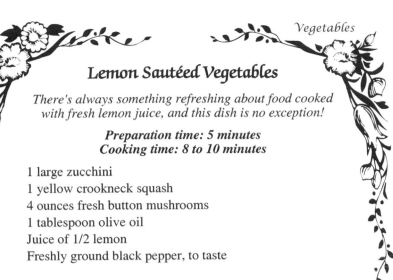

Lemon Sautéed Vegetables

There's always something refreshing about food cooked with fresh lemon juice, and this dish is no exception!

Preparation time: 5 minutes
Cooking time: 8 to 10 minutes

1 large zucchini
1 yellow crookneck squash
4 ounces fresh button mushrooms
1 tablespoon olive oil
Juice of 1/2 lemon
Freshly ground black pepper, to taste

Slice vegetables. Heat olive oil in sauté pan over medium-high heat. Add sliced vegetables, lemon juice, and black pepper. Sauté vegetables until done, stirring frequently. Serve hot.

Makes 4 servings

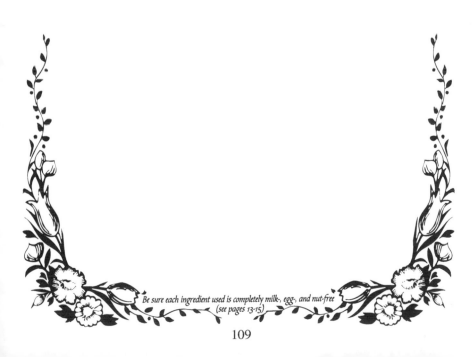

Be sure each ingredient used is completely milk-, egg-, and nut-free
(see pages 13-15)

Maple Glazed Vegetables

A great dish for a cold evening.

Preparation time: 15 to 20 minutes
Cooking time: 1 hour 5 minutes

1 medium Russet potato
1 large sweet potato
4 large carrots
1 medium onion
1/3 cup 100% pure **maple syrup**
1/4 cup packed brown sugar
1 teaspoon **vanilla extract**
1/2 teaspoon ground nutmeg
1/4 teaspoon ground cinnamon
2 tablespoons dairy-free **margarine**, cut into small pieces

Preheat oven to 400 degrees F.

Peel Russet potato and sweet potato and cut each into 1/2 inch chunks. Peel carrots and cut into 1/2 inch pieces. Peel onion and cut into 1/2 inch chunks. Place prepared vegetables in a large mixing bowl.

Combine maple syrup, brown sugar, vanilla extract, nutmeg and cinnamon in a small mixing bowl. Add maple syrup mixture to prepared vegetables; toss well to coat vegetables.

Place coated vegetables in 9" x 13" baking dish. Scatter margarine pieces over top. **Cover tightly with foil** and bake in preheated 400 degree oven for 45 minutes. **Remove foil** and stir the vegetables. Bake an additional 20 minutes uncovered, until the vegetables are softened and lightly browned. Serve hot.

Makes 4 to 6 servings

Be sure each ingredient used is completely milk-, egg-, and nut-free
(see pages 13-15)

Mixed Vegetables with Herbed Mustard Sauce

A delicious combination of flavors.

Preparation time: 20 minutes
Cooking time: 35 minutes

Vegetables:

- 2 small red potatoes, cut into 1/2-inch pieces
- 2 cups small broccoli florets
- 2 cups small cauliflower florets
- 1 small zucchini, cut into 1/8-inch-thick slices
- 1 cup sliced carrots (1/8-inch-thick slices)
- 1 (8 ounce) package fresh button mushrooms, cut into 1/8-inch-thick slices
- ½ cup sliced leek (1/8-inch-thick slices)

Sauce:

- 1/4 cup **Dijon mustard**
- 1/4 cup water
- 3 tablespoons olive oil
- 2 tablespoons freshly squeezed lemon juice
- 1 teaspoon crumbled dried basil leaves
- 1 teaspoon crumbled dried oregano leaves
- 1 teaspoon dried thyme leaves
- freshly ground black pepper, to taste

Prepare vegetables. Place steamer in 4 quart pot, and add water until the water barely touches the bottom of the steamer. Cover pot and bring water to a boil over high heat. Add potatoes, broccoli, cauliflower, zucchini, and carrots to steamer. Reduce heat to simmer; steam the vegetables, covered, for 20 minutes. Add mushrooms and leeks to pot. Cover and steam for another 15 minutes or until all vegetables are cooked. Drain vegetables and place in large serving bowl.

To prepare sauce, place all sauce ingredients in a small bowl and mix with a fork until well blended. Pour sauce over hot vegetables in serving bowl, and gently stir until all the vegetables are coated with the sauce. Serve hot.

Makes 9 servings (3/4 cup each)

Be sure each ingredient used is completely milk-, egg-, and nut-free (see pages 13-15)

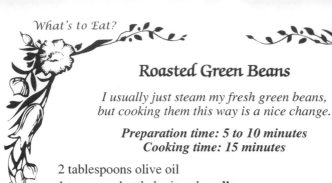

Roasted Green Beans

*I usually just steam my fresh green beans,
but cooking them this way is a nice change.*

**Preparation time: 5 to 10 minutes
Cooking time: 15 minutes**

2 tablespoons olive oil
1 teaspoon bottled minced **garlic**
1/2 teaspoon crumbled dried basil leaves
1/2 teaspoon crumbled dried oregano leaves
1 pound fresh green beans

Preheat oven to 450 degrees F.

In a small bowl or measuring cup, mix together olive oil,
garlic, basil, and oregano.

Wash and trim green beans, and cut into 1-inch-long pieces.
Place prepared green beans in 9" x 13" baking pan. Pour olive
oil mixture over beans; toss to coat. Spread green beans
evenly in pan. Bake, uncovered, in preheated 450 degree
oven for 15 minutes or until tender, stirring once during
cooking time.

Makes 4 servings

*Be sure each ingredient used is completely milk-, egg-, and nut-free
(see pages 13-15)*

Sautéed Vegetable Medley

*This simple and attractive dish can be multiplied
to make as many servings as you need.*

Preparation time: under 5 minutes
Cooking time: under 5 minutes

1 small zucchini, cut in half lengthwise and then sliced
8 fresh button mushrooms, sliced
1/4 small red bell pepper, chopped
1 green onion, chopped (including green top)
1 tablespoon dairy-free **margarine**
freshly ground black pepper, to taste

Prepare all vegetables.

Heat margarine in a small sauté pan over medium heat. Add
prepared vegetables and black pepper; sauté for 4 to 5 minutes
or until done. Serve hot.

Makes 2 servings

*Be sure each ingredient used is completely milk-, egg-, and nut-free
(see pages 13-15)*

113

Notes

Miscellaneous

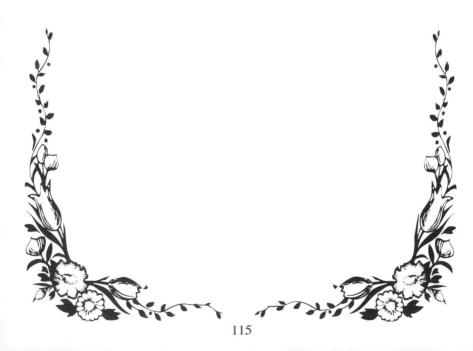

Cornbread Stuffing

*Making this stuffing is somewhat of a project,
but it's well worth it! You could use this to stuff into a
turkey, but I always prefer to cook my stuffings
in a separate dish.*

Preparation time: 20 minutes
Cooking time: 30 minutes
plus Cornbread preparation

1 recipe Corn Bread (see Corn Muffin recipe on page 131), cooked, cooled, and crumbled

3 cups dairy-, egg-, and nut-free fresh **French bread** (including crusts), torn into small pieces

1/2 medium green or red bell pepper

3 celery stalks

1 small onion

1 tablespoon dairy-free **margarine**

1 cup water

2 teaspoons **poultry seasoning**

1 teaspoon dried parsley flakes

1/2 teaspoon garlic salt

1/2 teaspoon black pepper

Preheat oven to 325 degrees F.

Place crumbled corn bread and torn French bread into a large mixing bowl; set aside.

Place vegetables into food processor that has been fitted with metal blade; process until vegetables are finely chopped.

Heat margarine in 10-inch sauté pan over medium-high heat. Add chopped vegetables and cook for 5 minutes, stirring often. Remove pan from heat.

In a measuring cup, stir together water and seasonings. Add cooked vegetables and seasoned water to breads in mixing bowl; mix well. Spoon mixture into oven-proof 7-cup casserole dish. Bake, uncovered, in preheated 325-degree oven for 30 minutes. Serve hot.

Makes 8 servings (3/4 cup each)

Be sure each ingredient used is completely milk-, egg-, and nut-free (see pages 13-15)

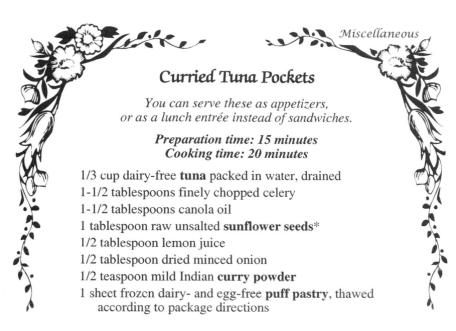

Curried Tuna Pockets

You can serve these as appetizers,
or as a lunch entrée instead of sandwiches.

Preparation time: 15 minutes
Cooking time: 20 minutes

1/3 cup dairy-free **tuna** packed in water, drained
1-1/2 tablespoons finely chopped celery
1-1/2 tablespoons canola oil
1 tablespoon raw unsalted **sunflower seeds***
1/2 tablespoon lemon juice
1/2 tablespoon dried minced onion
1/2 teaspoon mild Indian **curry powder**
1 sheet frozen dairy- and egg-free **puff pastry**, thawed
   according to package directions

Preheat oven to 400 degrees F. Lightly spray a baking sheet
with dairy-free non-stick **cooking spray**.

In a medium bowl, mix together all ingredients except puff
pastry sheet.

Open up puff pastry sheet; roll it into a 12-inch square. Cut
pastry sheet into 12 rectangles. Place a spoonful of the tuna
mixture into the center of each square. Moisten the edges of
the squares with water. Fold in half; seal edges with a fork.
Place on prepared baking sheet. Bake in preheated 400 degree
oven for 20 minutes, or until golden.

Makes 12

* Available at Natural Foods stores. Be sure to avoid roasted
sunflower seeds, as most commercially available roasted
sunflower seeds are roasted in peanut oil!

Be sure each ingredient used is completely milk-, egg-, and nut-free
(see pages 13-15)

Dash of Peach Barbecue Sauce

This sauce is sweet with just a hint of peach taste.

Preparation and cooking time: 5 minutes

1 (6 ounce) can **tomato paste**
1 (4 ounce) jar **pureed peaches** (i.e. baby food)
1/4 cup honey
1/4 cup **apple cider vinegar**
1 tablespoon **Dijon mustard**
1 tablespoon dairy-, egg-, and nut-free salt-free **seasoning blend**, such as "Mrs. Dash®"

Place all ingredients in a small saucepot. Cook over medium-low heat, stirring constantly, for 2 minutes. Remove from heat. Either use the sauce immediately or refrigerate until ready to use.

Makes 1-1/2 cups sauce

Be sure each ingredient used is completely milk-, egg-, and nut-free
(see pages 13-15)

Dilled Mustard Sauce

Serve this very simple sauce over steamed or sautéed fresh vegetables, or with potatoes.

Preparation time: 3 minutes

2 tablespoons water
1 tablespoon **Dijon mustard**
1 tablespoon **Sherry wine**
1/2 teaspoon dried dill weed
1/8 teaspoon salt
freshly ground black pepper, to taste

Place all ingredients in a small bowl or a measuring cup; mix well with a fork. Toss with hot, cooked vegetables or potatoes.

Makes 1/4 cup sauce

Be sure each ingredient used is completely milk-, egg-, and nut-free
(see pages 13-15)

Festive Tuna Swirls

These appetizers look attractive and taste delicious.

Preparation time: 12 to 15 minutes
Cooking time: 20 minutes

1 sheet frozen dairy- and egg-free **puff pastry**, thawed
   according to package directions
1 (6-1/2 ounce) can dairy-free **tuna** packed in water,
   drained
1/4 cup chopped green onions, including green tops
1/4 cup chopped red bell pepper
1 tablespoon olive oil
1/2 teaspoon dill

Preheat oven to 425 degrees F.

In a medium bowl, mix together tuna, chopped green onions,
chopped red bell pepper, olive oil and dill. Unfold pastry
sheet on a clean cutting board. Spread tuna mixture evenly
over pastry. Starting at one side, roll up like a jelly roll.
Using a sharp knife, cut into 1/2-inch slices. Place slices flat
(i.e. so that the "swirl" pattern shows) on an ungreased baking
sheet, 2 inches apart. Bake in preheated 425 degree oven for
20 minutes or until golden.

Makes approximately 17 appetizers

Be sure each ingredient used is completely milk-, egg-, and nut-free
(see pages 13-15)

Fresh Fruit Smoothie

I often make this delicious smoothie with breakfast. The recipe is easily multiplied, and works well with a wide variety of fruits and juices. Just be sure to include a banana and some type of frozen fruit, and it's bound to turn out great.

Preparation time: 5 minutes

1 medium-sized banana
1 cup whole frozen strawberries (frozen without sugar)
1 cup orange juice

Place all ingredients in blender. Blend on high until fruit is pureed and smoothie is smooth and well-blended.
Serve immediately.

Makes 2-1/2 cups

Be sure each ingredient used is completely milk-, egg-, and nut-free (see pages 13-15)

Shish Kebab Marinade

*This marinade is especially delicious when used with beef.
Try grilling beef kebobs made with cubes of marinated
London Broil skewered with onion pieces, mushrooms,
and other vegetables of your choice.*

Preparation time: 3 minutes

1/4 cup Balsamic vinegar
2 tablespoons dairy-, egg-, and nut-free **Worcestershire Sauce**
2 tablespoons Burgundy wine
1 tablespoon freshly squeezed lemon juice
freshly ground black pepper, to taste

Combine all ingredients in a medium mixing bowl.

Makes 1/2 cup of marinade

*Be sure each ingredient used is completely milk-, egg-, and nut-free
(see pages 13-15)*

Spinach Dip

I have served this creamy dip with tortilla chips at parties, and my guests couldn't believe that it was dairy-free.

Preparation time: 10 minutes
Chilling time: 1 hour

1/2 cup chopped red onion

1 (14 ounce) package regular **Tofu,** drained

1 (10 ounce) box frozen chopped spinach, thawed and drained

1/4 cup dairy- egg- and nut-free "**eggless mayonnaise**" (available in natural foods stores)

1-1/2 teaspoons bottled minced **garlic**

1 teaspoon lemon juice

1 teaspoon crumbled dried basil leaves

1 teaspoon crumbled dried oregano leaves

3/4 teaspoon salt

generous amount freshly ground black pepper

Using a food processor that has been fitted with the metal blade, finely chop the red onion. Add tofu and process one minute, pausing once to scrape the edges of the work bowl. Add all other ingredients to the tofu onion mixture in the food processor. Process for 30 seconds, pause to scrape the edges of the work bowl, and then process for another 15 seconds. Refrigerate for at least 1 hour; serve cold.

Makes 3 cups of dip

Be sure each ingredient used is completely milk-, egg-, and nut-free (see pages 13-15)

Sunflower Pesto

This thick pesto is a bit tricky to mix into pasta, but it's worth the effort. I think this is as close to the taste of a traditional pesto that you can get without using nuts and cheese!

Please note that pesto sauce is not cooked, and is not very good when "reheated" the next day. When I have leftover pasta pesto, my preference is to eat it cold rather than reheated.

Preparation time: 5 minutes

1 cup packed fresh basil leaves, washed
1/2 cup raw unsalted **sunflower seeds***
1/2 cup olive oil
2 teaspoons bottled minced **garlic**
1/2 teaspoon salt
freshly ground black pepper, to taste

Place all ingredients in a food processor that has been fitted with a metal blade. Process approximately 2 minutes -- until basil leaves are chopped fine, sunflower seeds are ground up, and mixture has formed a thick sauce. Scrape down the sides of the food processor bowl and process for another 20 seconds.

To make pasta pesto, toss freshly made pesto with freshly cooked and drained pasta, and then serve immediately.

Makes 1 cup pesto sauce
(enough to serve with a 12-ounce package of pasta)

* Available at Natural Foods stores. Be sure to avoid roasted sunflower seeds, as most commercially available roasted sunflower seeds are roasted in peanut oil!

Be sure each ingredient used is completely milk-, egg-, and nut-free (see pages 13-15)

Tangy Stir-Fry Sauce

When stir-frying, be sure to avoid using a wok that has previously been "seasoned" with peanut oil.

Preparation time: 3 to 5 minutes

1/4 cup plus 2 tablespoons dairy-free **soy sauce**
2 tablespoons tomato **ketchup**
2 tablespoons dry sherry
2 teaspoons bottled minced **garlic**
2 teaspoons sugar
1 teaspoon ground ginger

In a small bowl, mix together all ingredients. Use as a sauce while stir-frying shrimp, chicken, or vegetables. It tastes best if cooked with the dish rather than being added to the food after it is cooked.

Makes over 1/2 cup sauce

Be sure each ingredient used is completely milk-, egg-, and nut-free
(see pages 13-15)

Tuna and Vegetable Casserole

This colorful casserole is a perennial favorite with my family, especially my oldest son. Jason loves the taste, and I love to see him eat his vegetables!

Preparation time: 15 to 20 minutes
Cooking time: 30 minutes

3 cans (6-1/2 ounces each) dairy-free **tuna** packed in water, drained

3 medium carrots, peeled and sliced

1 medium zucchini, cut into lengthwise quarters and then sliced

1 yellow crookneck squash, cut into lengthwise quarters and then sliced

1 cup fresh pea pods or fresh green beans, trimmed and cut into 1 inch long pieces

1/2 small red bell pepper, chopped

3 green onions, chopped (including green tops)

1/4 cup dairy-free **margarine**, melted

1 tablespoon freshly squeezed lemon juice

1 teaspoon bottled minced **garlic**

1 teaspoon chopped dried dill weed

freshly ground black pepper, to taste

Preheat oven to 450 degrees F.

Place tuna in 9" x 15" casserole dish. Using a fork, break tuna into small pieces and spread evenly in dish. Prepare all vegetables as described in ingredient list. Layer vegetables in the casserole on top of the tuna, sprinkling vegetables evenly in dish, working in the order listed above (i.e. the carrots are placed on top of the tuna, the zucchini is on top of the carrots, etc.).

Combine melted margarine, lemon juice, minced garlic, dill weed, and pepper in small measuring cup. Pour evenly over casserole. Cover casserole tightly with aluminum foil and bake in preheated 450 degree oven for 30 minutes. Serve hot, over rice.

Makes 6 servings

Be sure each ingredient used is completely milk-, egg-, and nut-free
(see pages 13-15)

Quick Breads & Breakfast Foods

Apricot Cornbread Rounds

The end product of this recipe is not quite cornbread and not quite a biscuit, so I have settled on the name "cornbread rounds." Try them instead of rolls with dinner, or serve with breakfast or brunch.

Preparation time: 10 to 15 minutes
Cooking time: 12 to 15 minutes

1 cup **flour**
1 cup **cornmeal**
2 tablespoons sugar
1 tablespoon **baking powder**
1 teaspoon salt
1 cup chopped dried apricots
1/3 cup vegetable oil
1/3 cup orange juice
2 tablespoons water

Preheat oven to 350 degrees F.

In a large bowl, mix together the flour, cornmeal, sugar, baking powder, salt, and dried apricots. Add vegetable oil, orange juice, and water; mix well.

Knead dough 15 to 20 times on a floured board. Pat the dough on the floured board until it is 1/2-inch thick. Using a cookie cutter or an overturned glass, cut the dough into 2-1/2-inch circles. Place rounds on an ungreased cookie sheet. Bake in preheated 350 degree oven for 12 to 15 minutes or until the tops are golden brown. Serve immediately, with **apricot jam**, dairy-free **margarine**, or honey.

Note: As with biscuits, these taste best straight from the oven. Plan to serve them right away, as they are not very good cold.

Makes 11 (2-1/2-inch diameter) "rounds"

Be sure each ingredient used is completely milk-, egg-, and nut-free (see pages 13-15)

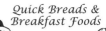

Baking Powder Biscuits

*This makes a wonderful old-fashioned biscuit. My children
and I like to cut these out with simple-shaped cookie cutters
(such as hearts for Valentine's Day) for a fun treat.*

Preparation time: 10 minutes
Cooking time: 10 to 12 minutes

2 cups **flour**
1 tablespoon sugar
1 tablespoon **baking powder**
1 teaspoon salt
2/3 cup water
1/3 cup vegetable oil

Preheat oven to 450 degrees F.

In a large bowl, mix together the flour, sugar, baking powder,
and salt. Set aside. In a 1-or 2-cup measuring cup, mix the
water and oil together; add to dry mixture and mix well.

Knead dough 20 to 25 times on a floured board. Roll or pat
the dough on a floured board until it is 1/2-inch thick. Using
a cookie cutter or an overturned glass, cut the dough into
2-inch circles; place on ungreased cookie sheet. Bake in
preheated 450 degree oven for 10 to 12 minutes or until the
tops are golden brown. Serve hot, with **jam**, honey, or
dairy-free **margarine**.

Makes 11 or 12 (2-inch diameter) biscuits

Variations:
Raisin and Spice Biscuits

Add ½ cup raisins, ½ teaspoon ground cinnamon, ½ teaspoon
ground nutmeg, and an additional 2 tablespoons sugar to basic
baking powder biscuit recipe. Prepare and bake as described
above, adding the extra ingredients to the dry mixture before
the oil and water are added.

Savory Italian Biscuits
A delicious accompaniment for an Italian-themed meal.

Add ½ teaspoon crumbled dried oregano leaves, ½ teaspoon
crumbled dried basil leaves, ½ teaspoon dried parsley
flakes, and ½ teaspoon crumbled dried rose-mary to basic
baking powder biscuit recipe. Prepare and bake as
described above, adding the extra ingredients to the dry
mixture before the oil and water are added.

*Be sure each ingredient used is completely milk-, egg-, and nut-free
(see pages 13-15)*

Cinnamon Roll Biscuits

*I remember the first time I tried this recipe. My kids and I
sat and ate the entire batch, one biscuit after another, as an
after-school treat. If you want, you can drizzle these with a
powdered sugar-and-water glaze after they come out of the
oven, but for my taste they're sweet enough as is.*

Preparation time: 15 minutes
Cooking time: 12 to 15 minutes

2 cups **flour**
2 tablespoons sugar
1 tablespoon **baking powder**
1/2 teaspoon salt
1 teaspoon **vanilla extract**
1/3 cup vegetable oil
2/3 cup water
1/4 cup dairy-free **margarine**, melted
1/4 cup packed brown sugar
1 teaspoon ground cinnamon

Preheat oven to 450 degrees F.

Mix together the flour, sugar, baking powder, and salt. Set
aside. In a 1- or 2-cup measuring cup, mix the oil and water
together. Add vanilla and oil-and-water mixture to the dry
mixture; mix until blended. Knead dough 20 to 25 times on a
floured board.

Roll the dough into a ¼-inch thick rectangle, approximately
11 inches x 14 inches. In a small bowl, mix the melted
margarine with the brown sugar and cinnamon. Spread brown
sugar mixture evenly over dough rectangle. Roll dough up
jelly-roll fashion, so that you end up with one 14-inch long
roll of dough. Pinch long end of roll closed so that it doesn't
come unrolled.

Slice dough roll into 1-inch wide slices. Place slices into
ungreased cupcake tins, 1 slice per hole, so that the spirals
show. Bake in preheated 450 degree oven for 12 to 15
minutes, until golden brown. Remove to serving platter; serve
warm.

Makes 15 small cinnamon roll biscuits

*Be sure each ingredient used is completely milk-, egg-, and nut-free
(see pages 13-15)*

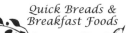

Corn Muffins

Preparation time: 12 minutes
Cooking time: 25 to 30 minutes
Cooling time: 20 minutes

1/2 cup dairy-free **margarine**, room temperature
1/4 cup sugar
3 tablespoons vegetable oil, 3 tablespoons water, and
    1-1/2 teaspoons **baking powder**, mixed together
1/2 cup water
1 cup **flour**
3/4 cup yellow **cornmeal**
2 teaspoons **baking powder**
1 teaspoon **baking soda**
1/4 teaspoon salt

Preheat oven to 350 degrees F. Line 12 regular muffin cups
with paper muffin liners.

In a large mixing bowl cream together margarine and sugar.
Add oil-water-baking powder mixture and all other ingredients
(including remaining 1/2 cup water and 2 teaspoons baking
powder) to margarine mixture; mix just until well blended.
Do not over-mix.

Spoon batter into prepared muffin tins, filling each one 2/3
full. Bake in preheated 350 degree oven for 25 to 30 minutes,
until muffins are golden brown. **Allow to cool 20 minutes**
before serving (they are very crumbly when hot).

Makes 12 muffins

Variation:
Corn Bread

Preparation time: 8 minutes
Cooking time: 25 to 30 minutes
Cooling time: 20 minutes

Using 100% vegetable **shortening**, grease and then
flour an 8-inch square baking pan.

Prepare batter as above. Pour batter into prepared
pan. Bake in preheated 350 degree oven for 25 to 30
minutes, until golden brown. Cool in pan 20
minutes. Cut into 9 squares. Serve.

Makes 9 servings

Be sure each ingredient used is completely milk-, egg-, and nut-free
(see pages 13-15)

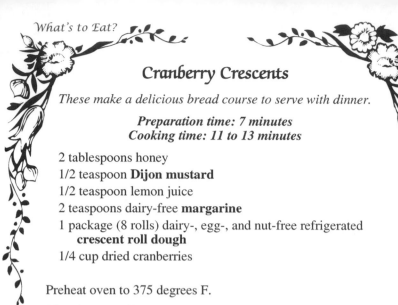

Cranberry Crescents

These make a delicious bread course to serve with dinner.

Preparation time: 7 minutes
Cooking time: 11 to 13 minutes

2 tablespoons honey
1/2 teaspoon **Dijon mustard**
1/2 teaspoon lemon juice
2 teaspoons dairy-free **margarine**
1 package (8 rolls) dairy-, egg-, and nut-free refrigerated **crescent roll dough**
1/4 cup dried cranberries

Preheat oven to 375 degrees F.

Place honey, Dijon mustard, lemon juice, and margarine in small sauce pot. Cook, over low heat, stirring constantly, until margarine melts. Remove from heat.

Open up crescent roll dough and separate into 8 triangles. Using a pastry brush, brush the top side of each triangle with the honey-mustard sauce. Sprinkle 1/2 tablespoon dried cranberries on each triangle. Roll up each triangle, starting at shortest side and rolling to opposite point; then gently curve into a crescent shape. Place crescents on ungreased cookie sheet; brush tops with remaining honey-mustard sauce. Bake in preheated 375 degree oven for 11 to 13 minutes, until golden brown. Serve warm.

Makes 8 rolls

Be sure each ingredient used is completely milk-, egg-, and nut-free (see pages 13-15)

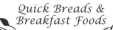

Iced Apple Breakfast Cake

This makes a very attractive cake that is dense and delicious.

Preparation time: 25 minutes
Cooking time: 40 minutes

1-1/3 cups packed brown sugar

1/2 cup dairy-free **margarine**, room temperature

2 (4 ounce) jars pureed **peaches** (i.e. babyfood)

1/3 cup orange juice

2 cups **flour**

1 tablespoon **baking powder**

2 cups (uncooked) quick-cooking **oats**

1/2 cup water

2 medium Granny Smith apples

1 tablespoon sugar

1/2 teaspoon cinnamon

2/3 cup sifted powdered sugar

1 tablespoon water

Preheat oven to 400 degrees F. Spray a 9-1/2-inch Springform (i.e. removable bottom) cake pan with dairy-free non-stick **cooking spray**.

In a large mixing bowl, cream together brown sugar and margarine. Stir in pureed peaches and orange juice. Add flour and baking powder; mix well. Stir in oats; mix well. Press half of dough mixture evenly into prepared pan.

Peel, core, and chop apples. In a medium bowl, mix 1 tablespoon sugar with 1/2 teaspoon cinnamon. Toss apples with cinnamon-sugar mixture.

Spoon apple mixture over dough in pan. Stir 1/2 cup water into remaining dough mixture to form a batter. Spoon batter evenly over apples. Bake in preheated 400 degree oven for 40 minutes or until done. Let cool for 30 minutes. Remove the removable side from the Springform pan.

To make icing, mix powdered sugar with 1 tablespoon water. Drizzle icing over cake. Serve.

Makes 8 servings

Be sure each ingredient used is completely milk-, egg-, and nut-free
(see pages 13-15)

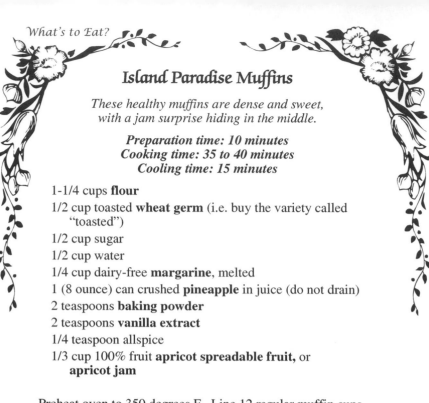

Island Paradise Muffins

*These healthy muffins are dense and sweet,
with a jam surprise hiding in the middle.*

Preparation time: 10 minutes
Cooking time: 35 to 40 minutes
Cooling time: 15 minutes

1-1/4 cups **flour**

1/2 cup toasted **wheat germ** (i.e. buy the variety called
  "toasted")

1/2 cup sugar

1/2 cup water

1/4 cup dairy-free **margarine**, melted

1 (8 ounce) can crushed **pineapple** in juice (do not drain)

2 teaspoons **baking powder**

2 teaspoons **vanilla extract**

1/4 teaspoon allspice

1/3 cup 100% fruit **apricot spreadable fruit,** or
  apricot jam

Preheat oven to 350 degrees F. Line 12 regular muffin cups
with paper muffin liners.

Place all ingredients except apricot spread in a large mixing
bowl; mix well.

Spoon batter into prepared muffin cups, filling each one 1/4
full. Spoon 1 teaspoon apricot spread into center of each
muffin; top with remaining batter (filling each muffin
almost full).

Bake in preheated 350 degree oven for 35 to 40 minutes, until
lightly browned and cooked through. Cool 15 minutes before
serving. Refrigerate any leftovers.

Makes 12 muffins

*Be sure each ingredient used is completely milk-, egg-, and nut-free
(see pages 13-15)*

Jam Surprise Muffins

These jam-filled muffins have a cake-like texture.

Preparation time: 12 to 15 minutes
Cooking time: 25 minutes

1-1/2 cups **flour**
3/4 cup sugar
2 teaspoons **baking powder**, divided use
1 teaspoon **baking soda**
1/2 teaspoon salt
1/4 cup dairy-free **margarine**, melted
3/4 cup water
2 teaspoons **vanilla extract**
2 tablespoons orange juice
3 tablespoons **jam** or **preserves** (any flavor)

Preheat oven to 350 degrees F. Line 10 regular muffin cups
with paper muffin liners.

In a large mixing bowl, combine flour, sugar, 1 teaspoon
baking powder, baking soda, salt, melted margarine, water,
and vanilla extract; mix until just blended. In a small bowl or
measuring cup mix 2 tablespoons orange juice with remaining
1 teaspoon baking powder until fizzy; add to batter mixture.
Mix until smooth and well-blended.

Spoon batter into each prepared muffin cup, filling each cup
1/4 full. Spoon 1 teaspoon jam into center of each muffin; top
with remaining batter. Bake in preheated 350 degree oven for
approximately 25 minutes, until cooked through. Remove
muffins from muffin cups and cool on wire rack 10 minutes
before serving.

Makes 10 muffins

Be sure each ingredient used is completely milk-, egg-, and nut-free
(see pages 13-15)

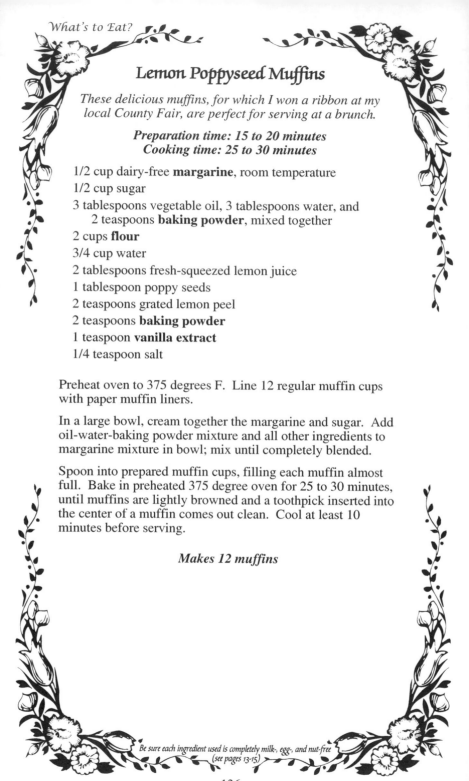

Lemon Poppyseed Muffins

These delicious muffins, for which I won a ribbon at my local County Fair, are perfect for serving at a brunch.

Preparation time: 15 to 20 minutes
Cooking time: 25 to 30 minutes

1/2 cup dairy-free **margarine**, room temperature
1/2 cup sugar
3 tablespoons vegetable oil, 3 tablespoons water, and
    2 teaspoons **baking powder**, mixed together
2 cups **flour**
3/4 cup water
2 tablespoons fresh-squeezed lemon juice
1 tablespoon poppy seeds
2 teaspoons grated lemon peel
2 teaspoons **baking powder**
1 teaspoon **vanilla extract**
1/4 teaspoon salt

Preheat oven to 375 degrees F. Line 12 regular muffin cups with paper muffin liners.

In a large bowl, cream together the margarine and sugar. Add oil-water-baking powder mixture and all other ingredients to margarine mixture in bowl; mix until completely blended.

Spoon into prepared muffin cups, filling each muffin almost full. Bake in preheated 375 degree oven for 25 to 30 minutes, until muffins are lightly browned and a toothpick inserted into the center of a muffin comes out clean. Cool at least 10 minutes before serving.

Makes 12 muffins

Be sure each ingredient used is completely milk-, egg-, and nut-free
(see pages 13-15)

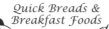

Pancakes

This pancake recipe has been a big hit among the members of my food allergy support group. I've been told that they also cook up well using rice milk instead of soy milk. I recommend you make a double batch, refrigerate or freeze the extras, and then reheat them in your toaster oven for a quick breakfast another day.

Preparation time: 5 minutes
Cooking time: approximately 15 minutes

1-1/2 cups **flour**
2-1/2 tablespoons sugar
3 teaspoons **baking powder**
2/3 cup vanilla flavored **soy milk**
3/4 cup water
2-1/2 tablespoons water, 2-1/2 tablespoons vegetable oil, and 1-1/2 teaspoons **baking powder**; mixed together

Place all ingredients in a medium mixing bowl and mix together until batter is smooth and well mixed.

Heat a large <u>non-stick</u> skillet over medium-high heat. Spoon batter into skillet, forming approximately 4-inch diameter pancakes. Cook until bubbles form and then pop over entire pancake, then turn over. Cook until second side is browned to desired doneness. Repeat with successive batches until all batter is used. Serve hot, with dairy-free **margarine**, dairy-free **pancake syrup**, or **jam.**

Makes about 11 (4-inch diameter) pancakes

Variation:

Blueberry Pancakes

Add 1 cup washed and drained fresh blueberries to the batter. Cook as above.

Pineapple Upside-Down Biscuits

My son Kevin and I love these, and so did the judges of Kretschmer Wheat Germ's "Easy and Delicious" Recipe Contest, who awarded it an Honorable Mention.

Preparation time: 15 minutes
Cooking time: 17 minutes

1 (8 ounce) can crushed **pineapple**, thoroughly drained

3 tablespoons dairy-free **margarine**, melted

1/3 cup packed brown sugar

½ teaspoon ground cinnamon

1 cup **flour**

½ cup toasted **wheat germ** (i.e. buy the variety called "toasted")

3 tablespoons sugar

3 teaspoons **baking powder**

½ teaspoon salt

½ cup water

¼ cup vegetable oil

Preheat oven to 450 degrees F.

In a small mixing bowl, combine drained pineapple, melted margarine, brown sugar and cinnamon. Spread this mixture evenly in an 8-inch-square baking dish. Set aside.

In large mixing bowl, mix together the flour, wheat germ, sugar, baking powder, and salt. Add water and vegetable oil and mix well. Knead dough 20 to 25 times on a floured board. Roll or pat the dough on a floured board until it is 1/2-inch thick. Using a cookie cutter or an overturned glass, cut the dough into nine 2-inch-diameter biscuits. Place biscuits in single layer on top of prepared pineapple mixture in baking dish.

Bake approximately 17 minutes, or until the tops are golden brown. Cool in pan for 2 minutes and then carefully invert onto serving platter. Separate into individual biscuits. Serve warm.

Makes 9 (2-inch diameter) biscuits

Be sure each ingredient used is completely milk-, egg-, and nut-free (see pages 13-15)

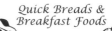
Raspberry Whole Wheat Muffins

An adventure in flavors!

Preparation time: 15 minutes
Cooking time: 30 minutes

1/2 cup dairy-free **margarine**, room temperature

1/3 cup sugar

3 tablespoons vegetable oil, 3 tablespoons water, and
    2 teaspoons **baking powder**, mixed together

1-1/2 cups **whole wheat flour**

1/2 cup toasted **wheat germ** (i.e. buy the variety called
    "toasted")

2 teaspoons **baking powder**

1/4 teaspoon salt

1/2 cup water

1 (10 ounce) package frozen raspberries with sugar, thawed
    (but <u>not</u> drained)

Preheat oven to 375 degrees F. Line 17 regular muffin cups
with paper muffin liners.

In a large bowl, cream together margarine and sugar. Add oil-
water-baking powder mixture, whole wheat flour, wheat germ,
remaining 2 teaspoons baking powder, salt, remaining 1/2 cup
water, and raspberries (with sugar syrup) to margarine
mixture; mix with wooden spoon until completely blended.
Note: the raspberries will break up into pieces during the
mixing process.

Spoon batter into prepared muffin cups, filling each muffin
3/4 full. Bake in preheated 375 degree oven for approximately
30 minutes, until muffins appear cooked and a toothpick
inserted into the center of muffin comes out clean.
Let cool before serving.

Makes 17 muffins

Be sure each ingredient used is completely milk-, egg-, and nut-free
(see pages 13-15)

Waffles

*Serve these up with dairy-free **margarine** and
pure **maple syrup** for a breakfast treat!*

**Preparation time: 5 minutes
Cooking time: 5 to 6 minutes per batch**

3 cups **flour**

1/4 cup sugar

3 teaspoons **baking powder**

1-1/3 cups vanilla flavored **soy milk**

1 cup water

1/4 cup vegetable oil, 1/4 cup water, and 3 teaspoons
   baking powder, mixed together

Oil waffle iron (either spray with dairy-free non-stick **cooking
spray**, or brush with vegetable oil). Preheat according to
manufacturer's directions.

Place all ingredients in large mixing bowl; mix well with
wire whisk.

Pour batter into hot, oiled waffle iron and cook until done,
approximately 5 to 6 minutes per batch. Repeat until all batter
is used.

Makes 16 (4-inch square) waffles

*Be sure each ingredient used is completely milk-, egg-, and nut-free
(see pages 13-15)*

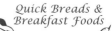

Wheat Germ
Baking Powder Biscuits

These biscuits are a little sweeter and a little healthier
than my basic Baking Powder Biscuit recipe
(See page 129).

Preparation time: 10 minutes
Cooking time: 12 minutes

1-2/3 cups **flour**

½ cup toasted **wheat germ** (i.e. buy the variety called
"toasted")

2 tablespoons sugar

1 tablespoon **baking powder**

½ teaspoon salt

2/3 cup water

1/3 cup vegetable oil

Preheat oven to 450 degrees F.

In a large bowl, mix together the flour, wheat germ, sugar,
baking powder, and salt. In a 1- or 2-cup measuring cup, mix
the water and oil together; add to dry mixture and mix well.

Knead dough 20 to 25 times on a floured board. Roll the
dough on a floured board until it is ½-inch thick. Using a
cookie cutter or an overturned glass, cut dough into 2-inch
circles; place on ungreased cookie sheet.

Bake for approximately 12 minutes, or until done. Serve hot,
with honey, **jam**, or dairy-free **margarine**.

Makes 15 (2-inch diameter) biscuits

Be sure each ingredient used is completely milk-, egg-, and nut-free
(see pages 13-15)

Whole Grain-Style Waffles

These hearty and filling waffles are one of my favorites.
Any leftovers can be reheated in a toaster the next day.

Preparation time: 5 minutes
Cooking time: about 7 minutes per batch

2 cups quick-cooking **oats**, uncooked
1 cup **flour**
2 teaspoons **baking powder**
2 tablespoons sugar
2-3/4 cups water
2 tablespoons vegetable oil

Oil waffle iron (either spray with dairy-free non-stick **cooking spray,** or brush with vegetable oil.) Do not skip this step -- these waffles sometimes even stick to waffle irons with "non-stick" finishes. Preheat waffle iron to hottest setting.

Place oats in food processor that has been fitted with the metal blade. Process until oats are ground into a coarse flour. Place ground oats and all other ingredients into a large bowl and mix well.

Pour batter into hot, oiled waffle iron and cook until done. Note: these waffles usually take 2 to 3 minutes longer to cook than the cooking time recommended by the waffle iron manufacturer.

Makes 12 to 13 (4-inch square) waffles

Variation:

Blueberry Waffles

Add 1 cup fresh or thawed and drained frozen blueberries to waffle batter. Prepare as above, adding 2 additional minutes to cooking time.

Be sure each ingredient used is completely milk-, egg-, and nut-free
(see pages 13-15)

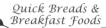

Whole Wheat Pumpkin Bread

*For me, the smell of pumpkin bread wafting through
the house heralds the arrival of fall. This recipe seems to
have become part of the annual Thanksgiving Feast
at my son's preschool, as well!*

Preparation time: 20 minutes   Cooking time: 1 hour

2/3 cup dairy-free **margarine**, room temperature

2 cups sugar

1 (15 ounce) can solid pack **pumpkin**

1 cup orange juice

1/3 cup vegetable oil, 1/3 cup water, and 3 teaspoons
  baking powder, mixed together

3 cups **whole wheat flour**

1 cup **flour**

1 tablespoon **baking powder**

2 teaspoons **baking soda**

2 teaspoons ground cinnamon

2 teaspoons ground cloves

Preheat oven to 350 degrees F. Using 100% **vegetable
shortening**, grease and then flour two 9-inch loaf pans.

Place margarine and sugar in large mixing bowl. Using
electric beaters on high speed, cream together until light and
fluffy. Add pumpkin, orange juice, and oil-water-baking
powder mixture; beat on medium speed until blended. Add
rest of ingredients; beat on low speed until well-blended.

Pour batter into prepared loaf pans. Bake in preheated 350
degree oven for 1 hour, or until toothpick inserted into the
middle of the loaf comes out clean. Cool for 15 minutes in
pans, and then turn out onto wire rack to cool completely.

Makes 2 (9-inch) loafs

Variation:

Big Batch Pumpkin Muffins

**Preparation time: 20 to 25 minutes
Cooking time: 25 minutes**

Prepare batter as above. Line 36 regular muffin cups with
paper muffin liners. Spoon batter into muffin cups, filling
each one almost full. Bake in preheated 350 degree oven for
25 minutes, or until toothpick inserted into center of muffin
comes out clean.

Makes 36 muffins

*Be sure each ingredient used is completely milk-, egg-, and nut-free
(see pages 13-15)*

Zucchini Bread

This zucchini bread is sweet, dense and very moist.

Preparation time: 10 minutes
Cooking time: 1 hour 10 minutes

- 2 cups finely grated zucchini
- 1 (8 ounce) can crushed **pineapple** packed in juice, thoroughly drained
- 1/3 cup raisins
- 2-1/4 cups **flour**
- 1 cup sugar
- 1 teaspoon **baking soda**
- 1-1/2 teaspoons **vanilla extract**
- 1/3 cup water
- 2 tablespoons vegetable oil (in addition to vegetable oil listed below)
- 3 tablespoons vegetable oil, 3 tablespoons water, and 2 teaspoons **baking powder**, mixed together

Preheat oven to 400 degrees F. Using 100% **vegetable shortening**, grease and then flour one 9" loaf pan.

Place all ingredients in a large mixing bowl. Mix with a wooden spoon until well mixed. Pour batter into prepared loaf pan. Bake in preheated 400 degree oven for approximately 1 hour and 10 minutes, until top of loaf is golden brown and a toothpick inserted into the center of the loaf comes out clean.

Cool in loaf pan 10 minutes, and then turn out onto wire rack to cool completely.

Makes one (9-inch) loaf

Be sure each ingredient used is completely milk-, egg-, and nut-free
(see pages 13-15)

Cakes

Chocolate Chip Bundt Cake

This bundt cake is moist and chocolaty.
Preparation time: 10 minutes
Cooking time: 55 minutes

3 cups **flour**
1-1/2 cups sugar
2 teaspoons **baking soda**
1 teaspoon salt
2 cups water
1/2 cup vegetable oil
2 tablespoons distilled white vinegar
2 teaspoons **vanilla extract**
1 cup dairy-free **semi-sweet chocolate chips**, divided use
Chocolate Glaze (see recipe below)

Preheat oven to 350 degrees F. Using 100% **vegetable shortening**, grease and then flour a 12-cup Bundt pan.

Place flour, sugar, baking soda, and salt in a large bowl. Add water, vinegar, vegetable oil, and vanilla extract; beat with wire whisk until smooth. Using a wooden spoon, stir in 1/2 cup of chocolate chips.

Pour batter into prepared Bundt pan. Bake at 350 degrees for 10 minutes. Gently stir in remaining 1/2 cup of chocolate chips. Bake an additional 45 minutes, until cake is golden brown and wooden pick inserted into the middle of the cake comes out clean. Let cool in pan for 10 minutes, then invert onto serving dish. Cool until room temperature, and then glaze with Chocolate Glaze.

Makes 12 servings.

Chocolate Glaze

Preparation and cooking time: 8 minutes

1 square dairy-free unsweetened **baking chocolate**
1 cup powdered sugar
2 tablespoons water

Unwrap chocolate and place in a microwave-safe bowl. Microwave on high for 2 to 3 minutes to melt; stir until smooth. Sift powdered sugar into bowl with melted chocolate, add water, and mix well. Immediately spoon over top of cooled Chocolate Chip Bundt Cake, allowing glaze to drip down sides of cake. Glaze will harden as it cools.

Be sure each ingredient used is completely milk-, egg-, and nut-free (see pages 13-15)

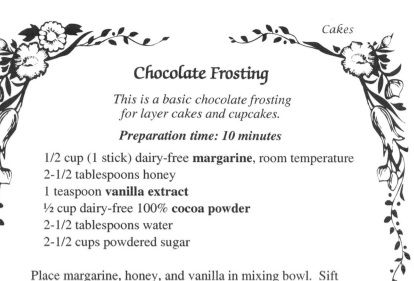

Chocolate Frosting

*This is a basic chocolate frosting
for layer cakes and cupcakes.*

Preparation time: 10 minutes

1/2 cup (1 stick) dairy-free **margarine**, room temperature
2-1/2 tablespoons honey
1 teaspoon **vanilla extract**
½ cup dairy-free 100% **cocoa powder**
2-1/2 tablespoons water
2-1/2 cups powdered sugar

Place margarine, honey, and vanilla in mixing bowl. Sift cocoa into this bowl. Using electric beaters at low speed, cream these ingredients together. Add water and sift powdered sugar into mixture. Beat with electric beaters on medium speed until well mixed. Use frosting to frost cake.

To assemble a layer cake: place one layer of cake in center of serving platter, upside down (so that the flat side of the cake, which was on the bottom of the cake pan, is facing you). Using a frosting spatula, spread top of this layer with frosting. Place remaining layer on top of this, right-side up. Spread frosting over top and sides of entire cake. Serve.

*Makes about 2-1/2 cups frosting,
enough to frost a 9-inch double-layer cake*

*Be sure each ingredient used is completely milk-, egg-, and nut-free
(see pages 13-15)*

Chocolate Layer Cake

This is my children's first pick for birthday cakes!

Preparation time: 10 to 13 minutes
Cooking time: 35 minutes

3 cups **flour**

2 cups sugar

1/2 cup dairy-free 100% **cocoa powder**

2 teaspoons **baking soda**

1 teaspoon salt

2 cups water

2/3 cup vegetable oil

2 tablespoons distilled white vinegar

2 teaspoons **vanilla extract**

Preheat oven to 350 degrees F. Using 100% **vegetable shortening**, grease and then flour two 9-inch round cake pans.

In a large mixing bowl, combine flour, sugar, cocoa, baking soda and salt. Add water, oil, vinegar and vanilla. Beat with a spoon or wire whisk just until batter is smooth and ingredients are well-blended.

Pour batter into prepared cake pans. Bake in preheated 350 degree oven for 35 minutes, or until wooden pick inserted into the center of the cake comes out clean. Let cool in pans 10 minutes before turning out onto wire racks to cool completely. Frost.

Makes one 9-inch round double-layer cake

Variations:
Chocolate Cupcakes

Prepare batter as above. Line 24 regular cupcake tins with paper cupcake liners. Fill cupcakes almost full. Bake in preheated 350 degree oven for 20 minutes or until done. Let cool on wire racks and then frost.

Makes 24 cupcakes

Chocolate Sheet Cake

Using 100% **vegetable shortening**, grease and then flour a 9-inch by 13-inch cake pan. Prepare batter as above; pour batter into prepared pan. Bake in preheated 350 degree oven for 35 minutes or until done. Let cool in pan 10 minutes before turning out onto serving platter to cool completely. Frost.

Makes one 9"x13" cake

Be sure each ingredient used is completely milk-, egg-, and nut-free (see pages 13-15)

Kevin's Strawberry Layer Cake

One day while we were playing at the park, my son Kevin said to me, "Why can't you make a strawberry flavored cake, with strawberry frosting?" "Let's do it!" I said, and the result was this delightful pink-frosted layer cake.

Preparation time: 10 minutes
Cooking time: 25 minutes

3 cups **flour**	1-1/4 cups water
1 cup sugar	1/3 cup vegetable oil
2 teaspoons **baking soda**	2 teaspoons **vanilla extract**
2 teaspoons **baking powder**	3 tablespoons distilled white vinegar
Kevin's Strawberry Frosting (see recipe below)	1-1/2 cups frozen strawberries (packed without sugar or liquid), thawed, divided use

Preheat oven to 400 degrees F. Using 100% **vegetable shortening**, grease and then flour two 9-inch round cake pans.

Place thawed strawberries in blender or food processor; puree (this should make approximately 2/3 cup of puree). Set aside 3 tablespoons of this puree to use in the frosting.

Sift together flour, sugar, baking soda, and baking powder into a large mixing bowl. Add strawberry puree (less the set-aside 3 tablespoonsful), water, vegetable oil, vinegar and vanilla extract to flour mixture. Beat well with a wire whisk.

Pour batter into prepared pans. Bake in preheated 400 degree oven for 25 minutes, or until toothpick inserted into center of cake comes out clean. Cool in pans for 10 minutes, and then turn out onto wire racks to cool completely. Frost with Kevin's Strawberry Frosting.

Makes one 9-inch layer cake (8 servings).

Kevin's Strawberry Frosting

Preparation time: 5 minutes
Frosting time: 5 to 10 minutes

1/2 cup dairy-free **margarine,** room temperature

3 cups powdered sugar

3 tablespoons strawberry puree (saved from above cake recipe)

1 teaspoon **vanilla extract**

Place margarine in medium mixing bowl. Sift in powdered sugar. Add strawberry puree and vanilla extract. Using electric beaters, beat at medium speed until light and fluffy. Use frosting to frost middle, top, and sides of layer cake.

Be sure each ingredient used is completely milk-, egg-, and nut-free
(see pages 13-15)

Linda's Luscious Coffee Cake

This moist and delicious cake looks especially attractive with its lattice-patterned icing.

Preparation time: 10 to 12 minutes
Cooking time: 35 to 40 minutes

1/2 cup dairy-free **margarine**, room temperature
1/2 cup sugar
1/2 cup orange juice
1/2 cup pure **maple syrup**
1-1/2 cups **flour**
1 teaspoon **baking soda**
1/4 teaspoon salt
1/3 cup golden raisins
1/3 cup dried cranberries
Maple Icing (see recipe below)

Preheat oven to 400 degrees F. Using 100% **vegetable shortening,** grease and then flour a 9-inch-square baking pan.

In a large mixing bowl, cream together the margarine and sugar. Add orange juice, maple syrup, flour, baking soda, and salt; mix well. Stir in raisins and dried cranberries.

Pour mixture into prepared baking pan. Bake in preheated 400 degree oven for 35 to 40 minutes, or until top of cake is golden brown and a toothpick inserted into the center of the cake comes out clean. Cool in pan on wire rack for 15 minutes. Invert cake onto a serving platter and allow to cool completely before icing. Ice with Maple Icing (recipe follows). To serve, cut into 16 squares.

Makes 16 servings (2-1/4" x 2-1/4" each)

Maple Icing

Preparation and icing time: 5 minutes

1 cup powdered sugar
1 tablespoon pure **maple syrup**
1 tablespoon water

Sift powdered sugar into a medium mixing bowl. Add maple syrup and water; mix well.

Cut off the bottom corner of a clean plastic bag, making a hole approximately 1/8-inch in diameter. Pour the icing into this bag. Pipe the icing through the hole in the bag onto the cooled cake, forming a lattice pattern with the icing on the cake.

Be sure each ingredient used is completely milk-, egg-, and nut-free
(see pages 13-15)

Orange Chocolate Marble Layer Cake

Your guests will rave about this sophisticated and delectable layer cake.

Preparation time: 20 minutes
Cooking time: 35 minutes

2-1/3 cups **flour**
1-1/2 cups sugar
1-1/2 teaspoons **baking soda**
3/4 teaspoon salt
1-1/2 cups orange juice
1/2 cup vegetable oil
1-1/2 teaspoons vanilla extract
1/2 tablespoon finely grated orange peel
3/4 cup dairy-free **semi-sweet chocolate chips**, melted
Chocolate Frosting (see recipe on page 147)

Preheat oven to 350 degrees F. Using 100% **vegetable shortening**, generously grease and then flour two 9-inch round cake pans.

In a large mixing bowl, combine flour, sugar, baking soda and salt. Add orange juice, vegetable oil, and vanilla; beat with a wire whisk until batter is smooth. Place 1-1/2 cups of batter into a separate bowl. Stir grated orange peel into remaining batter in original bowl. Using a wooden spoon, stir melted chocolate into the 1-1/2 cups of batter in the second bowl.

Alternately spoon orange and chocolate batters into prepared cake pans. With a knife, cut through batters and gently mix and swirl to obtain a marble effect, being careful not to let the knife touch the bottom or edges of the pan. Bake in preheated 350 degree oven for 35 minutes, or until toothpick inserted into center of cake comes out clean. Cool in pans for 10 minutes, and then turn out onto wire racks to cool completely. Frost middle, top, and sides of layer cake with Chocolate Frosting.

Makes one 9-inch round double-layer cake

Be sure each ingredient used is completely milk-, egg-, and nut-free (see pages 13-15)

Peach Upside Down Cake

This makes a beautiful cake, perfect for serving to company.
I entered this in the "Low Cholesterol Cakes" category at my
local County Fair, and came home with a prize ribbon!

Preparation time: 20 minutes
Cooking time: 35 minutes

3 tablespoons dairy-free **margarine**
1/3 cup firmly packed dark brown sugar
1 (15 ounce) can **Libby's® Lite sliced peaches***, reserve juice
1-1/2 cups **flour**
1/2 cup sugar
2 teaspoons **baking powder**
1/4 teaspoon salt
1 teaspoon **vanilla extract**
3 tablespoons vegetable oil, 3 tablespoons water, and 1-1/2
    teaspoons **baking powder**, mixed together

Preheat oven to 350 degrees F.

Place margarine in 9-inch round cake pan. Place cake pan in hot
oven until margarine is melted, about 2 minutes. Remove pan from
oven. Sprinkle brown sugar evenly over margarine in cake pan.
Drain can of peaches, **reserving juice**. If any of the peach slices are
particularly fat, slice them in half lengthwise. Arrange peaches in a
circular pattern in a single layer in the cake pan, placing peach slices
on top of the brown sugar.

Place flour, sugar, baking powder, salt, 1/2 cup of the reserved juice
(if necessary, add enough water to equal 1/2 cup of liquid), vanilla,
and water-oil-baking powder mixture in large mixing bowl; mix until
batter is smooth and well blended. Note: batter will be thick.

Carefully spoon the batter into the cake pan, covering the peaches.
Don't worry if there's not quite enough batter to cover all of the
peaches – the batter will rise and spread as it cooks. Set the cake pan
on a large cookie sheet (to catch any drips). Bake in preheated 350
degree oven for approximately 35 minutes, until cake is golden
brown and firm to the touch, and a toothpick inserted at the center of
the cake comes out clean. Cool cake in pan 5 minutes, then carefully
invert onto serving platter. Let cool completely. After serving, cover
and refrigerate any leftovers.

Makes 8 servings

  * I have specified Libby's brand sliced peaches because they are
    canned in a blend of fruit juices, rather than in just pear juice as
    most brands are. Using this particular brand makes a big
    difference in the taste of the cake. If Libby's brand is not
    available in your area, look for peaches that are canned in
    a fruit juice blend.

Be sure each ingredient used is completely milk-, egg-, and nut-free
(see pages 13-15)

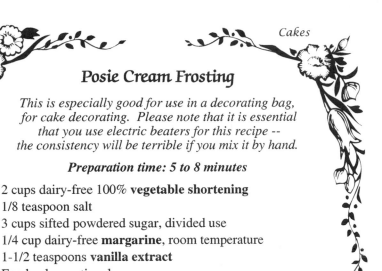

Posie Cream Frosting

*This is especially good for use in a decorating bag,
for cake decorating. Please note that it is essential
that you use electric beaters for this recipe --
the consistency will be terrible if you mix it by hand.*

Preparation time: 5 to 8 minutes

2 cups dairy-free 100% **vegetable shortening**
1/8 teaspoon salt
3 cups sifted powdered sugar, divided use
1/4 cup dairy-free **margarine**, room temperature
1-1/2 teaspoons **vanilla extract**
Food color, optional

Place shortening, salt, 1 cup of the powdered sugar, margarine
and vanilla in mixing bowl. Beat with electric beaters at
medium speed until mixture is smooth. Gradually beat in the
remaining sugar until of spreading consistency. If desired, tint
with food color.

*Makes enough frosting to frost a 9-inch double-layer cake
or a 9" x 13" single layer sheet cake, with enough left over
for decorating.*

*Be sure each ingredient used is completely milk-, egg-, and nut-free
(see pages 13-15)*

Spiced Blueberry Snack Cake

There is no need to frost this blueberry-filled cake.

Preparation time: 10 minutes
Cooking time: 30 minutes

1/2 cup dairy-free **margarine**, room temperature
1/2 cup packed brown sugar
1 cup **flour**
1 cup quick-cooking **oats**
2 teaspoons **baking powder**
1/2 teaspoon salt
1 teaspoon allspice
1 teaspoon ground cinnamon
3 tablespoons orange juice
2/3 cup thawed and drained frozen blueberries
1/2 cup **blueberry jam** or low-sugar **blueberry spreadable fruit**

Preheat oven to 350 degrees F. Using 100% **vegetable shortening**, lightly grease a 9-inch-square baking pan.

In a large mixing bowl, cream together margarine and brown sugar. Add flour, oats, baking powder, salt, allspice and cinnamon; mix well. Mixture will be crumbly. Set aside 3/4 cup of this crumbly dough. Add orange juice to the remaining dough. Gently fold blueberries into this dough.

Press blueberry dough mixture onto bottom of prepared pan. Using the back of a spoon, spread blueberry jam evenly over dough in pan. Sprinkle reserved crumbly dough evenly over jam. Bake in preheated 350 degree oven for 30 minutes, or until done. Cool in pan. Cut into 16 squares.

Makes 16 squares (2-1/4" x 2-1/4" each)

Tropical Pineapple-Glazed Cake

This makes a great finale for a Hawaiian-themed dinner!

Preparation time: 10 to 15 minutes
Cooking time: 30 minutes

Cake:

- 1-1/2 cups **flour**
- 1/2 cup sugar
- 1/4 cup packed brown sugar
- 3/4 cup water
- 1/4 cup vegetable oil
- 1/4 cup pineapple juice from canned pineapple that will be used in glaze
- 1 tablespoon distilled white vinegar
- 2 teaspoons **baking soda**
- 1 teaspoon **vanilla extract**

Glaze:

- 1 (8 ounce) can crushed **pineapple** in juice, drained, reserve juice
- 1/2 cup **apricot preserves** or low-sugar apricot **spreadable fruit**
- 1/4 cup packed brown sugar

Preheat oven to 375 degrees F. Using 100% **vegetable shortening**, grease and then flour one 9-inch round cake pan.

Place flour, sugar, 1/4 cup brown sugar, water, oil, pineapple juice, vinegar, baking soda and vanilla in mixing bowl; mix until batter is smooth.

Pour batter into prepared pan. Bake in preheated 375 degree oven for approximately 30 minutes, until a wooden pick inserted into the center of the cake comes out clean. Cool in pan 10 minutes, then invert onto serving platter.

To make glaze, place drained pineapple, apricot preserves and remaining 1/4 cup brown sugar in a small saucepan. Cook over medium heat, stirring constantly, until preserves are melted and bubbly. Slowly spoon the glaze evenly over the cake. Allow to cool completely before serving.

Makes 8 servings

Be sure each ingredient used is completely milk-, egg-, and nut-free
(see pages 13-15)

Vanilla Cake with Crumb Topping

My children wanted me to name this "Yummy Sugar Cake" because of its sweet, sugary topping. You can also use this batter to make a vanilla layer cake by omitting the crumb topping, doubling the cake ingredients, and baking at 400 degrees for 30 minutes in two 9-inch round cake pans. Either way, it's delicious!

Preparation time: 15 minutes
Cooking time: 30 minutes

Crumb Topping:
1/3 cup sugar
1/3 cup **flour**
½ teaspoon ground cinnamon
2 tablespoons chilled dairy-free **margarine**

Combine sugar, flour and cinnamon in a small mixing bowl. Using a pastry blender, cut in margarine until mixture resembles coarse crumbs. Set aside.

Cake:
1-1/2 cups **flour**
2/3 cup sugar
2 teaspoons **baking powder**
1 cup **vanilla-flavored soy milk**
¼ cup vegetable oil
1-1/2 tablespoons vegetable oil, 1-1/2 tablespoons water, 2 teaspoons **baking powder**; mixed together
1 teaspoon **vanilla extract**

Preheat oven to 400 degrees F. Using 100% **vegetable shortening**, grease and then flour a 10-inch round Springform baking pan (i.e. baking pan with removable sides).

Place all cake ingredients in a large mixing bowl; using a wire whisk, mix until well blended. Pour batter into prepared pan. Sprinkle crumb topping on top of batter. Bake for 30 minutes in preheated 400 degree oven, until a toothpick inserted into the center of the cake comes out clean. Cool cake in pan ten minutes, and then carefully remove the sides of the Springform pan. Cool completely before serving.

Makes 8 servings

Be sure each ingredient used is completely milk-, egg-, and nut-free (see pages 13-15)

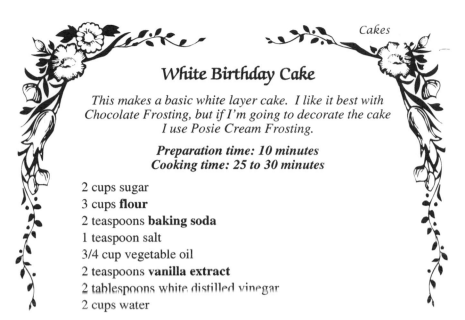

White Birthday Cake

This makes a basic white layer cake. I like it best with Chocolate Frosting, but if I'm going to decorate the cake I use Posie Cream Frosting.

Preparation time: 10 minutes
Cooking time: 25 to 30 minutes

2 cups sugar

3 cups **flour**

2 teaspoons **baking soda**

1 teaspoon salt

3/4 cup vegetable oil

2 teaspoons **vanilla extract**

2 tablespoons white distilled vinegar

2 cups water

Preheat oven to 350 degrees F. Using 100% **vegetable shortening**, grease and then flour two 9-inch round cake pans.

Sift dry ingredients together into large mixing bowl. Add remaining ingredients; beat with electric mixer at medium speed until smooth.

Pour batter into prepared cake pans. Bake in preheated 350 degree oven for 25 to 30 minutes, or until a wooden pick inserted into the middle of the cake comes out clean. Let cool in pans 10 minutes before turning out onto wire racks to cool completely. Frost.

Makes one 9-inch round double-layer cake

Be sure each ingredient used is completely milk-, egg-, and nut-free (see pages 13-15)

157

Notes

Cookies

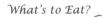

Always Delicious
Chocolate Chip Cookies

*These are always a hit at parties and picnics,
and they freeze well, too!*

Preparation time: 25 minutes
Cooking time: 10 minutes

1 cup dairy-free **margarine**, room temperature

3/4 cup sugar

3/4 cup firmly packed brown sugar

1 teaspoon **vanilla extract**

3 tablespoons vegetable oil, 3 tablespoons water, and
    1-1/2 teaspoons **baking powder**, mixed together

2-1/4 cups **flour**

1 teaspoon **baking powder**

1 teaspoon salt

2 cups dairy-free **semi-sweet chocolate chips**

Preheat oven to 375 degrees F.

In a large bowl, cream together margarine, sugar, brown sugar,
and vanilla extract. Add oil-water-baking powder mixture to
dough; mix well. Mix in flour, remaining 1 teaspoon baking
powder, and salt; mix until well blended. Stir in chocolate chips.

Form dough into 1-inch diameter balls. Place dough balls
approximately 2 inches apart on ungreased cookie sheets.
Bake in preheated 375 degree oven for about 10 minutes,
until golden brown. Cool on wire racks.

Makes 72 (2-inch diameter) cookies

Variation:
Chocolate Chip Cookie Bars

Preparation time: 15 minutes
Cooking time: 25 minutes

Using 100% **vegetable shortening**, grease a 9-inch
by 13-inch baking pan. Prepare dough as above.
Spread dough evenly in prepared baking pan. Bake
in preheated 375 degree oven for 20 to 25 minutes,
until done. Cool in pan, then cut into 32 squares.

*Makes 32 cookie bars
(approximately 1-1/2" x 2" each)*

*Be sure each ingredient used is completely milk-, egg-, and nut-free
(see pages 13-15)*

Apricot Blondies

*These sweet, rich cookies have a wonderful moist,
chewy, brownie-like texture.*

Preparation time: 10 minutes
Cooking time: 25 minutes

Cookie:

1/2 cup packed brown sugar
1/2 cup sugar
1/2 cup dairy-free **margarine**, room temperature
1 cup **flour**
1 cup quick-cooking **oats**
2 teaspoons **baking soda**
1/4 cup orange juice
1 teaspoon **vanilla extract**
1/3 cup chopped **dried apricots**

Icing:

1/2 cup sifted powdered sugar
1 tablespoon **apricot jam** or 100% fruit **apricot
spreadable fruit**
1 tablespoon orange juice

Preheat oven to 400 degrees F. Using 100% **vegetable
shortening**, grease an 8-inch-square baking pan.

In a large mixing bowl, cream together brown sugar, sugar,
and margarine. Using a wooden spoon, mix in flour, oats,
baking soda, 1/4 cup orange juice, vanilla extract, and
chopped dried apricots.

Press dough evenly into prepared pan. Bake in preheated 400
degree oven for 25 minutes, until dough is set. Do not
overcook. Cool in pan for 10 minutes.

To make icing, mix together powdered sugar, apricot jam,
and 1 tablespoon orange juice. Drizzle icing over cookies.
Cut into 16 squares. Let cool completely before serving.

Makes 16 (2" square) bars

*Be sure each ingredient used is completely milk-, egg-, and nut-free
(see pages 13-15)*

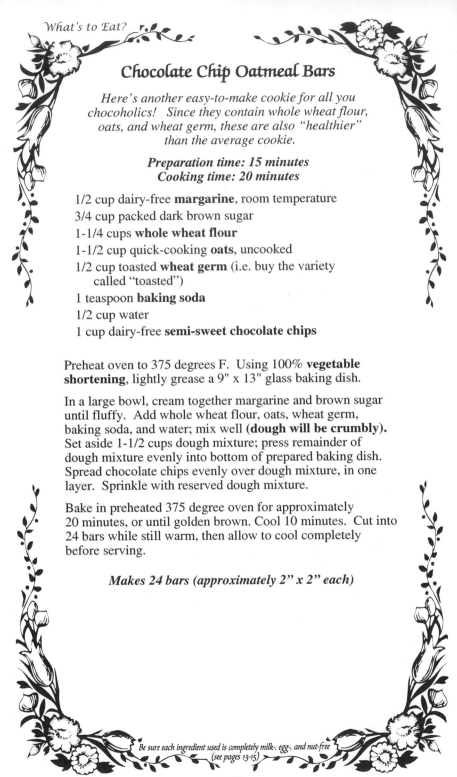

Chocolate Chip Oatmeal Bars

Here's another easy-to-make cookie for all you chocoholics! Since they contain whole wheat flour, oats, and wheat germ, these are also "healthier" than the average cookie.

Preparation time: 15 minutes
Cooking time: 20 minutes

1/2 cup dairy-free **margarine**, room temperature

3/4 cup packed dark brown sugar

1-1/4 cups **whole wheat flour**

1-1/2 cup quick-cooking **oats**, uncooked

1/2 cup toasted **wheat germ** (i.e. buy the variety called "toasted")

1 teaspoon **baking soda**

1/2 cup water

1 cup dairy-free **semi-sweet chocolate chips**

Preheat oven to 375 degrees F. Using 100% **vegetable shortening**, lightly grease a 9" x 13" glass baking dish.

In a large bowl, cream together margarine and brown sugar until fluffy. Add whole wheat flour, oats, wheat germ, baking soda, and water; mix well **(dough will be crumbly).** Set aside 1-1/2 cups dough mixture; press remainder of dough mixture evenly into bottom of prepared baking dish. Spread chocolate chips evenly over dough mixture, in one layer. Sprinkle with reserved dough mixture.

Bake in preheated 375 degree oven for approximately 20 minutes, or until golden brown. Cool 10 minutes. Cut into 24 bars while still warm, then allow to cool completely before serving.

Makes 24 bars (approximately 2" x 2" each)

Be sure each ingredient used is completely milk-, egg-, and nut-free (see pages 13-15)

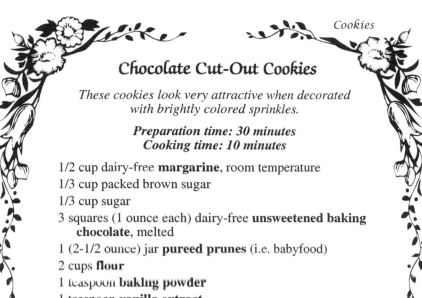

Chocolate Cut-Out Cookies

*These cookies look very attractive when decorated
with brightly colored sprinkles.*

Preparation time: 30 minutes
Cooking time: 10 minutes

1/2 cup dairy-free **margarine**, room temperature

1/3 cup packed brown sugar

1/3 cup sugar

3 squares (1 ounce each) dairy-free **unsweetened baking
   chocolate**, melted

1 (2-1/2 ounce) jar **pureed prunes** (i.e. babyfood)

2 cups **flour**

1 teaspoon **baking powder**

1 teaspoon **vanilla extract**

3 tablespoons vegetable oil, 3 tablespoons water, and
   1-1/2 teaspoons **baking powder**, mixed together

dairy-, egg-, and nut-free **colorful sprinkles**

In a large mixing bowl, cream together margarine, brown
sugar and sugar. Add melted chocolate and pureed prunes;
mix well. Add flour, 1 teaspoon baking powder, vanilla, and
oil-water-baking powder mixture; mix well.

Preheat oven to 350 degrees F.

Roll out dough on floured board to 1/4-inch thickness. Cut
out with cookie cutters; place cookies on ungreased cookie
sheets. Sprinkle cookies with colorful sprinkles. Bake in
preheated 350 degree oven for 10 minutes. Remove to wire
racks to cool.

Makes about 3 or 4 dozen cookies, depending on size

*Be sure each ingredient used is completely milk-, egg-, and nut-free
(see pages 13-15)*

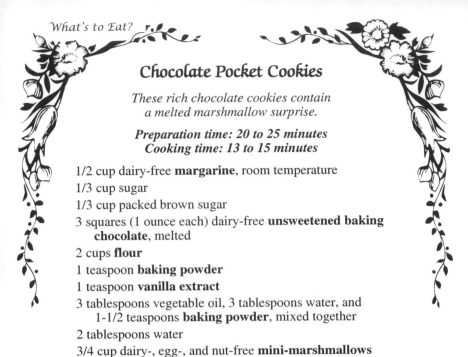

Chocolate Pocket Cookies

*These rich chocolate cookies contain
a melted marshmallow surprise.*

**Preparation time: 20 to 25 minutes
Cooking time: 13 to 15 minutes**

1/2 cup dairy-free **margarine**, room temperature

1/3 cup sugar

1/3 cup packed brown sugar

3 squares (1 ounce each) dairy-free **unsweetened baking chocolate**, melted

2 cups **flour**

1 teaspoon **baking powder**

1 teaspoon **vanilla extract**

3 tablespoons vegetable oil, 3 tablespoons water, and 1-1/2 teaspoons **baking powder**, mixed together

2 tablespoons water

3/4 cup dairy-, egg-, and nut-free **mini-marshmallows**

In a large mixing bowl, cream together margarine, sugar, and brown sugar. Stir in melted chocolate. Add flour, 1 teaspoon baking powder, vanilla, oil-water-baking powder mixture, and 2 tablespoons water; mix well.

Preheat oven to 350 degrees F.

Roll out dough on unfloured board to 1/4-inch thickness. Using a biscuit cutter or an overturned glass, cut dough into 3-inch diameter circles. If necessary, use a spatula to remove circles from board. Working quickly so that the dough does not dry out, place 4 mini-marshmallows on each circle. Fold each circle in half, tightly pinching edges closed to seal. Place 1 inch apart on ungreased cookie sheets.

Bake for 13 to15 minutes or until done. Remove to wire racks to cool before serving.

Makes 16 cookies

*Be sure each ingredient used is completely milk-, egg-, and nut-free
(see pages 13-15)*

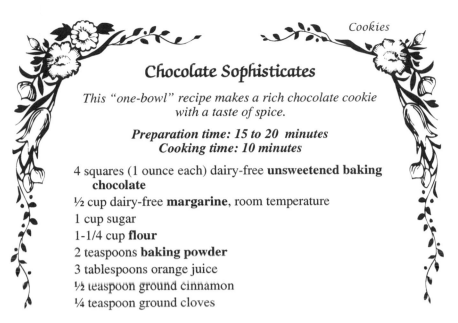

Chocolate Sophisticates

This "one-bowl" recipe makes a rich chocolate cookie with a taste of spice.

Preparation time: 15 to 20 minutes
Cooking time: 10 minutes

4 squares (1 ounce each) dairy-free **unsweetened baking chocolate**

½ cup dairy-free **margarine**, room temperature

1 cup sugar

1-1/4 cup **flour**

2 teaspoons **baking powder**

3 tablespoons orange juice

½ teaspoon ground cinnamon

¼ teaspoon ground cloves

Preheat oven to 350 degrees F.

Place chocolate in microwave-safe mixing bowl. Microwave on high until melted, 2 to 2-1/2 minutes, stirring after first minute. Stir until smooth.

Combine margarine and sugar with melted chocolate. Add flour, baking powder, orange juice, cinnamon, and cloves; mix well.

Form dough into 1-inch balls. Place balls approximately 2 inches apart on ungreased cookie sheets. Bake in preheated 350 degree oven for about 10 minutes. Cool on cookie sheets 1 minute, then remove to wire racks to cool completely.

Makes 38 cookies

Be sure each ingredient used is completely milk-, egg-, and nut-free (see pages 13-15)

Fiesta Chocolate Cookies

Very attractive, delicious chocolate cookies.

Preparation time: 20 minutes
Cooking time: 10 minutes

1/2 cup dairy-free **semi-sweet chocolate chips**

1-1/2 tablespoons vegetable oil, 1-1/2 tablespoons water,
    and 1 teaspoon **baking powder**, mixed together

1/2 cup dairy-free **margarine**, room temperature

1/4 cup sugar

1/2 teaspoon **vanilla extract**

1-1/2 cups **flour**

1 teaspoon **baking powder**

1/4 teaspoon salt

dairy-, egg-, and nut-free **colorful sprinkles** (specifically,
    the type that look like multi-colored straight lines)

Preheat oven to 350 degrees F.

Place chocolate chips in large microwaveable mixing bowl.
Cover with a paper towel and microwave on high for
3 minutes to melt; stir until smooth. Add oil-water-baking
powder mixture, margarine, sugar, and vanilla to melted
chocolate; beat with electric beaters at medium speed until
well blended. Add flour, remaining 1 teaspoon baking
powder, and salt; beat at medium speed until well blended.

Place colorful sprinkles on a small plate. Shape dough into
approximately 1-inch diameter balls. Roll the top half of each
dough ball in the sprinkles. Place balls, sprinkle side up,
2 inches apart on ungreased cookie sheets. Bake in preheated
350 degree oven for about 10 minutes; do not overcook, as
cookies will harden as they cool. Cool on wire racks. Store
cooled cookies in airtight container.

Makes about 36 cookies

Be sure each ingredient used is completely milk-, egg-, and nut-free
(see pages 13-15)

Frosted Maple Drops

Old-fashioned cookies with a delightful maple flavor.

Preparation time: 10 minutes
Cooking time: 12 minutes

1/2 cup dairy-free **margarine**, room temperature
1-1/4 cups **flour**
1/3 cup packed brown sugar
1/4 cup pure maple syrup
1-1/2 tablespoons vegetable oil, 1-1/2 tablespoons water,
   and 1 teaspoon **baking powder**, mixed together
Maple Frosting (see recipe below)

Preheat oven to 350 degrees F.

Place margarine, flour, brown sugar, maple syrup, and oil-water-baking powder mixture in a large mixing bowl. Using electric beaters, beat on medium speed until all ingredients are thoroughly mixed.

Drop dough by rounded teaspoonfuls, 2 inches apart, onto ungreased cookie sheets. Bake in preheated 350 degree oven for about 12 minutes, or until edges are firm. Remove to wire racks to cool. Frost with Maple Frosting.

Makes 35 cookies

Maple Frosting

Preparation and frosting time: 7 to 10 minutes

3 tablespoons 100% pure **maple syrup**
2 tablespoons dairy-free **margarine**, room temperature
1 cup sifted powdered sugar

In a medium mixing bowl, cream together maple syrup and margarine. Add sifted powdered sugar; mix well. Frost cookies.

Be sure each ingredient used is completely milk-, egg-, and nut-free (see pages 13-15)

Gimme S'More Cookie Bars

*These very sweet and rich cookie bars
are a real crowd pleaser!*

**Preparation time: 15 minutes
Cooking time: 25 minutes**

1 cup dairy-free **margarine**, room temperature

1-1/4 cups packed brown sugar

2 teaspoons **vanilla extract**

3 tablespoons vegetable oil, 3 tablespoons water, and
2 teaspoons **baking powder**, mixed together

2 cups **flour**

1 teaspoon **baking powder**

1/2 teaspoon salt

1-3/4 cups dairy- and egg-free **mini marshmallows**

1-1/3 cups dairy-free **semi-sweet chocolate chips**

5 (2-3/8" x 5" each) dairy-, egg-, and nut-free **graham
crackers**, broken into small pieces

Preheat oven to 375 degrees F. Using 100% **vegetable
shortening**, grease and then flour a 9-inch by 13-inch
baking pan.

In a large mixing bowl, cream together margarine and brown
sugar. Stir in vanilla and oil-water-baking powder mixture.
Add flour, remaining 1 teaspoon baking powder, and salt; mix
well. Fold in marshmallows, chocolate chips, and graham
cracker pieces.

Spread dough evenly in prepared pan. Bake in preheated 375
degree oven for approximately 25 minutes, or until golden
brown but still a little "soft" to the touch. Cool 10 minutes
(they will get harder as they cool). Cut into 32 bars while still
warm, then allow to cool completely before serving.

Makes 32 cookie bars (approximate 1-1/2" x 2" each)

*Be sure each ingredient used is completely milk-, egg-, and nut-free
(see pages 13-15)*

Gingerbread Cookies

*Get out your gingerbread man cookie cutter and
make some of these old-fashioned treats today!*

Preparation time: 20 minutes
Cooking time: 9 minutes

½ cup dairy-free **margarine**, room temperature
2/3 cup packed brown sugar
¼ cup molasses
3 tablespoons water
2 cups **flour**
2 teaspoons arrowroot powder*
1-1/2 teaspoons **baking powder**
1 teaspoon ground cinnamon
½ teaspoon ground ginger
icing (optional, see below)

Preheat oven to 375 degrees F.

In large mixing bowl, cream together margarine and brown
sugar. Add molasses, water, flour, arrowroot powder, baking
powder, baking soda, cinnamon and ginger; mix well.

Roll out dough on floured board to ¼-inch thickness. Cut out
with cookie cutters; place on ungreased cookie sheets. Bake
in preheated 375 degree oven for 9 minutes. Do not overcook,
as cookies will harden as they cool. Remove to wire racks
to cool.

Makes about 30 cookies, depending on size.

Optional Icing

Preparation and Icing time: 10 minutes

1-1/3 cups powdered sugar
1 tablespoon + 1 teaspoon water

Sift powdered sugar into a medium mixing bowl. Add water
and mix well.

Cut off the bottom corner of a clean plastic bag to make a hole
approximately 1/8-inch in diameter. Pour or spoon the icing
into this bag. Pipe the icing through the hole in the bag onto
the cooled cookies.

* Available in natural foods stores; sometimes
  available in the "spice" section of the supermarket.

Be sure each ingredient used is completely milk-, egg-, and nut-free
(see pages 13-15)

Hamantaschen

Here is a dairy- and egg-free version of the cookies traditionally served at the Jewish festival of Purim. The Hamantaschen's triangular shape is said to resemble the hat worn by Haman, the villain of the Purim story.

Preparation time: 25 to 30 minutes
Cooking time: 20 to 25 minutes

1/2 cup dairy-free **margarine**, room temperature

1/2 cup sugar

1/4 cup packed brown sugar

2 cups **flour**

1 teaspoon **baking powder**

3 tablespoons orange juice

1 teaspoon **vanilla extract**

3 tablespoons vegetable oil, 3 tablespoons water, and 1-1/2 teaspoons **baking powder**, mixed together

Jam (flavor of your choice), for filling

Preheat oven to 350 degrees F. Lightly spray cookie sheets with dairy-free non-stick **cooking spray** (do not use an olive oil-based spray, as this would negatively affect the flavor of the cookies).

In large mixing bowl, cream together margarine, sugar, and brown sugar. Add flour, 1 teaspoon baking powder, orange juice, vanilla extract, and oil-water-baking powder mixture; mix well.

Using a floured rolling pin, roll dough out half of dough on floured board to 1/4-inch thickness. Using a floured overturned glass or a floured cookie cutter, cut into 3-inch circles. Place circles on prepared cookie sheets. Place approximately 1/2 to 1 teaspoon jam in center of each circle. <u>Tightly</u> pinch together the sides of the circle to form a triangle shape, with the filling showing in the middle of the cookie. Repeat with remaining dough. Bake in preheated 350 degree oven for 20 to 25 minutes or until done.

Makes 28 cookies

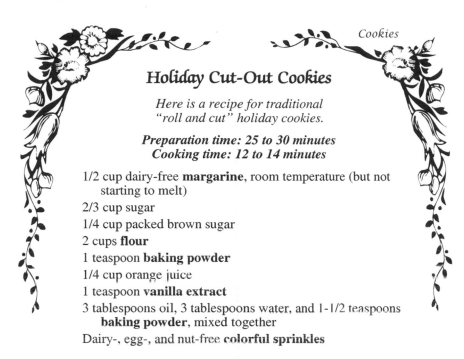

Holiday Cut-Out Cookies

*Here is a recipe for traditional
"roll and cut" holiday cookies.*

**Preparation time: 25 to 30 minutes
Cooking time: 12 to 14 minutes**

- 1/2 cup dairy-free **margarine**, room temperature (but not starting to melt)
- 2/3 cup sugar
- 1/4 cup packed brown sugar
- 2 cups **flour**
- 1 teaspoon **baking powder**
- 1/4 cup orange juice
- 1 teaspoon **vanilla extract**
- 3 tablespoons oil, 3 tablespoons water, and 1-1/2 teaspoons **baking powder**, mixed together
- Dairy-, egg-, and nut-free **colorful sprinkles**

In large mixing bowl, cream together margarine, sugar, and brown sugar. Stir in flour, 1 teaspoon baking powder, orange juice, vanilla, and oil-water-baking powder mixture; mix well.

Preheat oven to 350 degrees F.

Roll out dough on heavily floured board to 1/8-inch thick. Cut out with cookie cutters. If necessary, use a spatula to remove from board. Place one inch apart on ungreased cookie sheets and decorate with colorful sprinkles.

Bake in preheated 350 degree oven for 12 to 14 minutes. Remove to wire racks to cool.

Makes approximately 36 cookies, depending on size

Be sure each ingredient used is completely milk-, egg-, and nut-free (see pages 13-15)

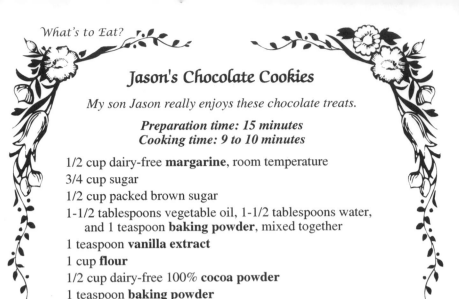

Jason's Chocolate Cookies

My son Jason really enjoys these chocolate treats.

Preparation time: 15 minutes
Cooking time: 9 to 10 minutes

1/2 cup dairy-free **margarine**, room temperature
3/4 cup sugar
1/2 cup packed brown sugar
1-1/2 tablespoons vegetable oil, 1-1/2 tablespoons water, and 1 teaspoon **baking powder**, mixed together
1 teaspoon **vanilla extract**
1 cup **flour**
1/2 cup dairy-free 100% **cocoa powder**
1 teaspoon **baking powder**

Preheat oven to 350 degrees F.

In a large mixing bowl, cream together margarine, sugar, and brown sugar. Mix in oil-water-baking powder mixture and vanilla. Add flour, cocoa, and baking powder; mix well.

Roll dough into 1-inch diameter balls; place balls 2 inches apart on ungreased cookie sheets.

Bake in preheated 350 degree oven for 9 to 10 minutes; do not overcook as cookies will harden as they cool. Cool on cookie sheets for 1 minute, and then remove to wire racks to cool completely.

Makes 36 cookies

Be sure each ingredient used is completely milk-, egg-, and nut-free (see pages 13-15)

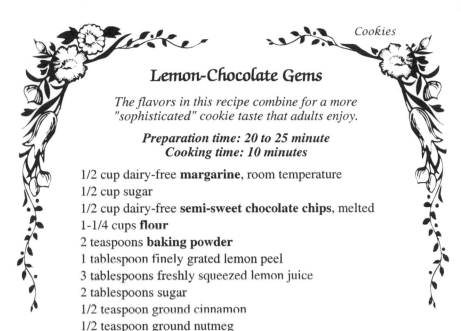

Lemon-Chocolate Gems

The flavors in this recipe combine for a more "sophisticated" cookie taste that adults enjoy.

Preparation time: 20 to 25 minute
Cooking time: 10 minutes

1/2 cup dairy-free **margarine**, room temperature
1/2 cup sugar
1/2 cup dairy-free **semi-sweet chocolate chips**, melted
1-1/4 cups **flour**
2 teaspoons **baking powder**
1 tablespoon finely grated lemon peel
3 tablespoons freshly squeezed lemon juice
2 tablespoons sugar
1/2 teaspoon ground cinnamon
1/2 teaspoon ground nutmeg

Preheat oven to 350 degrees F.

In a large mixing bowl, cream together margarine and 1/2 cup sugar. Stir in melted chocolate. Add flour, baking powder, grated lemon peel, and lemon juice; mix well.

In a small bowl, mix the remaining 2 tablespoons sugar with the cinnamon and nutmeg.

Roll dough into 1-inch balls. Roll each ball in sugar-cinnamon-nutmeg mixture to coat, and then place 2 inches apart on ungreased cookie sheets. Bake in preheated 350 degree oven for 10 minutes. Cool on cookie sheet for 1 minute, and then remove to wire rack to cool completely.

Makes 36 cookies

Be sure each ingredient used is completely milk-, egg-, and nut-free (see pages 13-15)

Lemon-Raspberry Bars

*These bars are more complex to make than most of
my cookie recipes, but are well worth the effort.*

Preparation time: 25 minutes
Cooking time: 30 minutes

Cookie:

1/4 cup dairy-free **margarine**, room temperature

1/2 cup powdered sugar

1 cup **flour**

1 tablespoon grated lemon peel

3 tablespoons freshly squeezed lemon juice

2 tablespoons water

1 teaspoon **baking powder**

Filling:

1/2 cup 100% fruit **raspberry spreadable fruit**

Topping:

1/4 cup flour

2 tablespoons sugar

2 tablespoons brown sugar

1 teaspoon grated lemon peel

2 tablespoons chilled dairy-free **margarine**

Preheat oven to 350 degrees F. Lightly spray a 9-inch-square baking
pan with dairy-free non-stick **cooking spray**.

To make cookie:
In a medium mixing bowl, cream together 1/4 cup margarine and
powdered sugar. Add remaining cookie ingredients and mix well.
Press mixture evenly into prepared pan.

To make filling:
Spread raspberry spread evenly over cookie mixture in pan.

To make topping:
Place 1/4 cup flour, 2 tablespoons sugar, 2 tablespoons brown
sugar, and 1 teaspoon grated lemon peel in small mixing bowl;
mix well. Using a pastry blender, cut in 2 tablespoons chilled
margarine until mixture resembles coarse crumbs. Sprinkle
evenly over raspberry spread in pan.

Bake in preheated 350 degree oven for 30 minutes or until
done. Cool in pan. Cut into 16 squares
(approximately 2-1/4" each).

Makes 16 bars (2-1/4" x 2-1/4" each)

*Be sure each ingredient used is completely milk-, egg-, and nut-free
(see pages 13-15)*

Oatmeal Cookies

*These incredible cookies are especially fabulous
fresh from the oven! I usually make a double batch,
because 3 dozen of these cookies just don't last very long
in my household.*

Preparation time: 12 to 15 minutes
Cooking time: 10 minutes

1/2 cup dairy-free **margarine**, room temperature

1/2 cup sugar

1/2 cup packed brown sugar

1-1/2 tablespoons vegetable oil, 1-1/2 tablespoons water,
   and 1 teaspoon **baking powder**, mixed together

1 teaspoon **vanilla extract**

1 tablespoon water

1 cup **flour**

1/2 teaspoon **baking soda**

1/2 teaspoon **baking powder**

1 cup quick cooking **oats**

Preheat oven to 350 degrees F.

In a large bowl, cream together margarine, sugar, and brown
sugar. Add oil-water-baking powder mixture and remaining
ingredients; mix well.

Drop dough by teaspoonfuls, 2 inches apart, onto ungreased
cookie sheets. Bake for 10 minutes or until lightly browned.
Cool on cookie sheets 1 minute before removing to wire racks
to cool completely.

Makes 36 cookies

Be sure each ingredient used is completely milk-, egg-, and nut-free
(see pages 13-15)

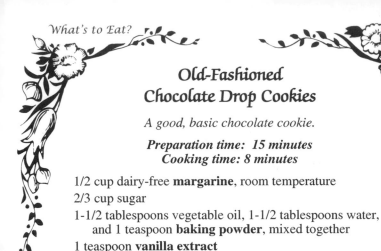

Old-Fashioned Chocolate Drop Cookies

A good, basic chocolate cookie.

Preparation time: 15 minutes
Cooking time: 8 minutes

1/2 cup dairy-free **margarine**, room temperature
2/3 cup sugar
1-1/2 tablespoons vegetable oil, 1-1/2 tablespoons water, and 1 teaspoon **baking powder**, mixed together
1 teaspoon **vanilla extract**
1-1/4 cups **flour**
3 tablespoons dairy-free 100% **cocoa powder**
1/4 teaspoon salt

Preheat oven to 375 degrees F.

In a large mixing bowl, cream together margarine and sugar. Add oil-water-baking powder mixture and vanilla; mix well. Add flour, cocoa, and salt; mix until well-blended.

Drop by teaspoonfuls, 2-inches apart, onto ungreased cookie sheets. Bake in preheated 375 degree oven for 8 to 10 minutes, until cooked but still soft in the center. Do not overcook – the cookies will harden some as they cool. Cool 1 minute on cookie sheets, then remove to wire racks to cool completely.

Makes about 30 cookies

Be sure each ingredient used is completely milk-, egg-, and nut-free (see pages 13-15)

Spritz Cookies

*Get out your cookie press to make these pretty,
not-too-sweet cookies.*

Preparation time: 30 minutes
Cooking time: 13 minutes

1 cup dairy-free **margarine**, room temperature
3/4 cup powdered sugar
2-1/4 cups **flour**
2 tablespoons water
1 teaspoon **vanilla extract**
1 tablespoon vegetable oil, 1 tablespoon water, and
   1 teaspoon **baking powder**, mixed together
1/2 cup dairy-free **semi-sweet chocolate chips**
2 teaspoons 100% **vegetable shortening**
(optional) dairy-, egg-, and nut-free **colorful sprinkles**

Preheat oven to 375 degrees F.

In a large mixing bowl, cream the margarine using electric
beaters at medium speed. Sift powdered sugar onto
margarine; cream together at medium speed. Sift flour onto
margarine mixture, add water, vanilla, and oil-water-baking
powder mixture. Beat at medium speed until well mixed.

Fill cookie press with cookie dough and form cookies onto
ungreased cookie sheets, placing cookies about 1 inch apart.
Bake in preheated 375 degree oven for approximately 13
minutes. Remove to wire racks to cool.

Place chocolate chips and shortening in microwave-proof
measuring cup. Microwave on high for 1 minute; stir.
Microwave on high for 1 more minute; stir until chocolate is
completely melted. Spoon melted chocolate onto middle of
each cookie; if desired, sprinkle chocolate with colorful
sprinkles. Allow chocolate to cool and harden before serving.

Makes 4-1/2 dozen cookies

*Be sure each ingredient used is completely milk-, egg-, and nut-free
(see pages 13-15)*

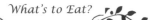

Sweet and Delicious Raisin Bars

*I'm not sure why, but there's something about these cookies
that for me always conjures up images of a sweet little
grandma lovingly baking cookies for her grandchildren.*

Preparation time: 20 minute
Baking time: 20-25 minutes

Filling:

1-1/2 cups dark raisins
¼ cup honey
2 tablespoons orange juice
1 tablespoon poppy seeds
1 tablespoon grated orange peel
½ teaspoon ground cinnamon

Dough:

½ cup dairy-free **margarine**, room temperature
½ cup firmly packed brown sugar
¼ cup sugar
2 cups **flour**
1/3 cup orange juice
2 teaspoons **baking powder**

Preheat oven to 375 degrees F. Lightly spray an 8" x 8"
square baking pan with dairy-free non-stick **cooking spray**.

Combine filling ingredients in a 1-1/2 quart pot. Bring to a
boil over medium-high heat, stirring frequently. Reduce
heat to low and simmer, uncovered, for 5 minutes. Remove
pot from heat and set aside.

Meanwhile, while the filling is simmering, prepare dough.
Cream together margarine and sugars in a large mixing
bowl. Add in flour, 1/3 cup orange juice, and baking
powder; mix well.

Press half of dough evenly onto bottom of prepared baking
pan. Top with prepared filling. Crumble remaining dough
evenly over filling. Bake in preheated 375 degree oven for
20 to 25 minutes or until done. Cut into 16 squares. Cool
completely before serving.

Makes 16 (2" square) bars

Be sure each ingredient used is completely milk-, egg-, and nut-free
(see pages 13-15)

Whole Wheat Chocolate Chip Cookies

This is a "healthier", less sweet chocolate chip cookie, for those who prefer a more "whole grain" taste.

Preparation time: 15 minutes
Cooking time: 10 to 12 minutes

2 tablespoons dairy-free **margarine**, room temperature
3 tablespoons honey
1/4 cup packed brown sugar
1-1/2 tablespoons water, 1-1/2 tablespoons vegetable oil, and 1-1/2 teaspoons **baking powder**, mixed together
1/4 cup unsweetened **applesauce**
1/2 teaspoon **vanilla extract**
1 cup **whole wheat flour**
1 teaspoon **baking powder**
1/8 teaspoon salt
1/4 cup quick-cooking **oats**
1 cup dairy-free **semi-sweet chocolate chips**

Preheat oven to 350 degrees F.

In a large bowl, cream together margarine, honey, and brown sugar. Add oil-water-baking powder mixture, vanilla, and applesauce; mix well. Add whole wheat flour, 1 teaspoon baking powder, and salt; mix well. Add oats and mix well with a wooden spoon. Stir in chocolate chips.

Drop dough by rounded teaspoonfuls two inches apart onto ungreased cookie sheets. Bake in preheated 350 degree oven for 10 to 12 minutes, until lightly browned. Remove to wire racks to cool.

Makes approximately 40 cookies

Be sure each ingredient used is completely milk-, egg-, and nut-free
(see pages 13-15)

Notes

Other Desserts

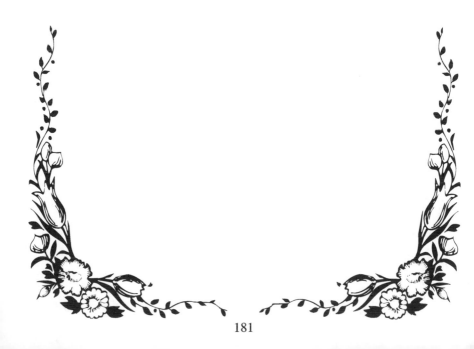

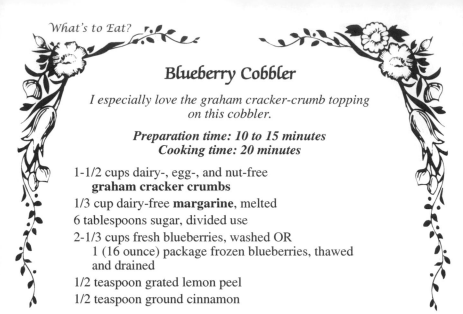

Blueberry Cobbler

I especially love the graham cracker-crumb topping on this cobbler.

Preparation time: 10 to 15 minutes
Cooking time: 20 minutes

1-1/2 cups dairy-, egg-, and nut-free
  graham cracker crumbs

1/3 cup dairy-free **margarine**, melted

6 tablespoons sugar, divided use

2-1/3 cups fresh blueberries, washed OR
  1 (16 ounce) package frozen blueberries, thawed
  and drained

1/2 teaspoon grated lemon peel

1/2 teaspoon ground cinnamon

Preheat oven to 425 degrees F. Using 100% **vegetable shortening**, lightly grease a 9-inch-square baking pan.

In a medium bowl, combine graham cracker crumbs, melted margarine, and 3 tablespoons sugar; mix well. Press half of this crumb mixture onto bottom of prepared baking pan. Set remaining crumb mixture aside.

Place blueberries, lemon peel, remaining 3 tablespoons sugar, and cinnamon in a separate medium bowl. Using a rubber spatula, gently toss the blueberries with the other ingredients until they are mixed. Spoon blueberry mixture evenly over crumb mixture in baking pan. Sprinkle remaining crumb mixture evenly over blueberries. Bake in preheated 425 degree oven for 20 minutes, until crumb topping is golden. Let cool 10 minutes and then cut into 9 pieces.

Serve warm. If desired, serve with non-dairy (such as soy- or rice-based) imitation vanilla **"ice cream"**.

Makes 9 servings (3" x 3" each)

Be sure each ingredient used is completely milk-, egg-, and nut-free
(see pages 13-15)

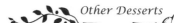

Blueberry Pear-adise Pie

The chopped pears in this pie are a perfect compliment to the blueberries.

Preparation time: 15 minutes
Cooking time: 40 minutes

1 (12 ounce) box frozen unsweetened blueberries; thawed, rinsed, and drained

2 fresh, firm Bartlett pears; peeled, cored and diced

2/3 cup sugar

1/3 cup flour

1/2 teaspoon ground cinnamon

Pie crust pastry for double-crusted pie
(see recipe on page 188)

Preheat oven to 425 degrees F.

Place all ingredients except pie crust pastry in a large mixing bowl. Using a rubber spatula, gently combine until well mixed.

Place bottom crust in ungreased 9-inch pie pan. Press crust firmly against sides and bottom of pan. Spoon blueberry-pear mixture into pie. Place top crust over filling. Roll the excess (i.e. overhanging) bottom crust up over the top crust edge, and press together to seal. Flute edges. Cut slits in top crust*. Bake in preheated 425 degree oven for 40 minutes or until done. Cool before serving. Store any leftover pie in refrigerator.

Makes 8 servings

* Note: to make a more decorative pie, I like to use a small heart-shaped cookie cutter to cut a pretty heart pattern in the top crust *before* I place the crust on the pie.

Be sure each ingredient used is completely milk-, egg-, and nut-free (see pages 13-15)

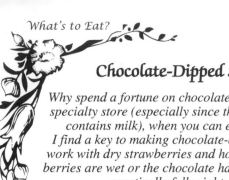

Chocolate-Dipped Strawberries

Why spend a fortune on chocolate-dipped strawberries at a
specialty store (especially since their chocolate most likely
contains milk), when you can easily make your own?
I find a key to making chocolate-dipped strawberries is to
work with dry strawberries and hot melted chocolate. If the
berries are wet or the chocolate has cooled off, the chocolate
practically falls right off the berries.

Preparation time: 15 minutes
Chilling time: 30 minutes

1 pint fresh strawberries
1 cup dairy-free **semi-sweet chocolate chips**
1 tablespoon dairy-free **vegetable shortening**

Line a cookie sheet with waxed paper. Wash strawberries, but do not remove green leaves. Pat dry with paper towels; set aside.

Place chocolate chips and shortening in a microwave-safe bowl. Cover with a paper towel and microwave on high for 3 to 3-1/2 minutes to melt; stir until smooth.

Using green tops as "handles," dip strawberries, one at a time, into the melted chocolate mixture, turning to coat. Place on prepared cookie sheet. Work quickly, because the chocolate won't "stick" to the strawberries when the chocolate cools off.

Refrigerate until chocolate is firm, approximately 30 minutes. Keep refrigerated until ready to serve; serve cold.

Makes approximately 4 servings

Be sure each ingredient used is completely milk-, egg-, and nut-free
(see pages 13-15)

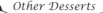

Chocolate Mousse

You'll be surprised by how rich and satisfying this tofu-based chocolate mousse is.

Preparation time: 7 minutes
Chilling time: 1 hour

3/4 cup dairy-free **semi-sweet chocolate chips**
1 (10.5 ounce) box light silken **Tofu**, extra firm*
1 teaspoon **vanilla extract**

Place chocolate chips in microwave-proof bowl. Cover with a paper towel and microwave on high for 2 minutes to melt; stir until smooth.

Crumble tofu into work bowl of food processor that has been fitted with the metal blade. Process until smooth and creamy, stopping to scrape down the edges of the work bowl with a spatula as necessary. Add melted chocolate chips and vanilla to tofu. Process until completely mixed, stopping to scrape down the edges of the work bowl with a spatula as necessary.

Spoon mousse into 4 small individual serving bowls. Chill for at least 1 hour before serving.

Makes 4 servings

* This type of tofu is available in natural foods stores and some supermarkets, and is packaged in a shelf-stable container that looks similar to a juice box.

Variation:
Chocolate Raspberry Mousse

Preparation time: 9 minutes
Chilling time: 1 hour

Place ½ cup **seedless raspberry 100% fruit spreadable fruit** in a microwavable measuring cup. Microwave for 30 seconds on high, or until melted. Prepare mousse as above, adding melted raspberry spreadable fruit to the tofu with the melted chocolate chips and the vanilla.

Makes 4 servings

*Be sure each ingredient used is completely milk-, egg-, and nut-free
(see pages 13-15)*

Fun Fruit

My kids named this treat "Fun Fruit" because there is something delightfully fun about the way the pieces of frozen fruit feel in your mouth. It makes a great snack or dessert for a hot summer's day.

Preparation time: 15 minutes
Freezing time: 1-1/2 hours

2 medium bananas, peeled
1 pint fresh strawberries, washed and hulled

Line a baking sheet with waxed paper. Slice fruit. Arrange sliced fruit in single layer on prepared baking sheet. Place in freezer for at least 1-1/2 hours.

Right before serving, remove frozen fruit slices from waxed paper and place in food processor that has been fitted with the metal blade. Process until fruit is chopped into very small pieces, but is not pureed. Serve immediately.

Makes 4 servings (1 cup each)

Be sure each ingredient used is completely milk-, egg-, and nut-free (see pages 13-15)

Lemony Apple Crisp

My youngest son and I love this recipe, which can easily be halved or doubled depending on how many people you are serving. However, just cook the amount you need for today's dessert -- by tomorrow the topping will be completely soggy and unappealing.

Preparation time: 10 to 15 minute
Cooking time: 25 minutes

1/4 cup **flour**
2 tablespoons sugar
2 tablespoons firmly packed brown sugar
1 teaspoon finely grated lemon peel
2 tablespoons chilled dairy-free **margarine**
5 medium-sized apples

Preheat oven to 350 degrees F.

Place flour, sugar, brown sugar, and lemon peel in a medium mixing bowl; mix well. Using a pastry blender, cut in chilled margarine until mixture resembles coarse crumbs. Set aside.

Peel and core apples. Chop apples into 1/2-inch or 3/4-inch chunks. Place chopped apples in 10-inch quiche pan. Sprinkle crumb mixture evenly over apples. Bake, uncovered, in preheated 350 degree oven for approximately 25 minutes. Cool in baking pan for 10 minutes. Serve warm.

Makes 4 servings

Be sure each ingredient used is completely milk-, egg-, and nut-free
(see pages 13-15)

Pie Crust Pastry

*This makes enough pastry for a double-crusted 9-inch pie. Fill it with your favorite **fruit pie filling**.*

Preparation time: 15 minutes

2 cups **flour**
1 teaspoon salt
2/3 cup dairy-free 100% **vegetable shortening**
6 to 8 tablespoons ice water

Mix together flour and salt in large mixing bowl. Using a pastry blender, cut in vegetable shortening until mixture resemble coarse crumbs. Mix in the ice water one tablespoon at a time, until the dough begins to form a ball. Dough should be moist enough to stick together without crumbling, but not overly wet.

Divide dough into two balls. Place first ball on a well-floured board; press down with the palm of your hand to flatten ball. Using a well-floured rolling pin, roll pastry dough into a ¼-inch thick circle that is big enough to fit in a 9-inch pie plate. Set aside, or set into 9-inch pie plate. Roll out second dough ball.

Make pie as per directions in pie recipe.

Makes enough pastry for a double-crusted 9-inch pie

Be sure each ingredient used is completely milk-, egg-, and nut-free (see pages 13-15)

Menu Ideas

*Don't forget to double-check the ingredients
on all purchased items!!*

__PARTIES__

Mother's Day Luncheon

Mediterranean Chicken (page 54)
Cool and Fresh Pasta Salad (page 75)
Corn on the Cob served with dairy-free margarine
Fresh Strawberries
(Purchased) dairy- and egg-free French Bread or Rolls
Orange Chocolate Marble Layer Cake (page 151)

Back-Yard Barbecue: Menu 1

Tortilla Chips served with Purchased Salsa
Basket of fresh seasonal fruit
Barbecued Chicken made with Dash of Peach Barbecue
    Sauce (page 118)
New Potatoes with Sun-Dried Tomato Dressing (page 91)
Corn on the Cob served with dairy-free margarine
Fresh Green Salad served with dairy- and egg-free Dressing
Cranberry Crescents (page 132)
Always Delicious Chocolate Chip Cookie Bars (page 160)
Oatmeal Cookies (page 175)

Back-Yard Barbecue: Menu 2

Tortilla Chips served with Spinach Dip (page 123)
Platter of raw fresh vegetables
    (such as carrot and celery sticks, etc.)
Beef Kabobs made with Shish Kebab Marinade (page 122)
Fruited Carrot Salad (page 25)
Tabbouleh Celebration (page 33)
Seasonal fresh fruits and melons
Baking Powder Biscuits (page 129), served with
    jam and dairy-free margarine
Fiesta Chocolate Cookies (page 166)
Frosted Maple Drops (page 167)

*Be sure each ingredient used is completely milk-, egg-, and nut-free
(see pages 13-15)*

Thanksgiving Dinner

Roasted Turkey with [Seasoned Baked Chicken]
  Seasoning Combination #3 (page 57)
Cornbread Stuffing (page 116)
Whipped Potatoes (page 95)
Canned Cranberry Sauce
Fresh steamed vegetables
Whole Wheat Pumpkin Bread (page 143)
Apple Pie, made with Pie Crust Pastry (page 188)
Blueberry Pear-adise Pie (page 183)

Slumber Party Breakfast

Pancakes (page 137)
Dairy-free Bacon
Fresh Fruit Smoothie (page 121)
Seasonal Fresh Fruit Salad

DINNER FOR GUESTS

Steak Dinner

Flank Steak with Mustard Sauce (page 40)
Baked Potatoes served with dairy-free margarine
Sautéed Vegetable Medley (page 113)
Chocolate Chip Bundt Cake (page 146)

Easy and Delicious

Sautéed Beef with Sun-Dried Tomato Sauce (page 44),
  over egg-free Angel Hair Pasta
Roasted Green Beans (page 112)
Chocolate-Dipped Strawberries (page 184)

Super Salmon

Salmon with Tomato and Herb Topping (page 72)
Bell Pepper Rice (page 100)
Fresh steamed green vegetables
Peach Upside Down Cake (page 152)

*Be sure each ingredient used is completely milk-, egg-, and nut-free
(see pages 13-15)*

FAMILY MEALS

Winter Supper

Creamy Sweet Potato Soup (page 21)
Fresh Green Salad served with dairy- and egg-free Dressing
Corn Muffins (page 131)

Jason's Choice

Orange Teriyaki Marinated Flank Steak (page 43)
White Rice
Fresh Green Salad served with dairy- and egg-free Dressing
Jason's Chocolate Cookies (page 172)

Sunday Dinner

Seasoned Baked Chicken (page 57)
Potato-Tomato Bake (page 93)
Fresh steamed green vegetables
Applesauce
Wheat Germ Baking Powder Biscuits (page 129),
    served with apricot jam
Kevin's Strawberry Layer Cake (page 149)

Hawaiian Theme

Chicken and Rice Luau (page 49)
Fresh Green Salad served with dairy- and egg-free Dressing
Tropical Pineapple-Glazed Cake (page 155)

Kid-Pleasing

Plum Crazy Chicken (page 56)
Spiced Apple Pasta (page 82)
Carrot and Celery Sticks
Chocolate Pocket Cookies (page 164)

Quick & Easy Fish

Pan-Fried Orange Roughy (page 69)
Basil Rice (page 99)
Lemon Sautéed Vegetables (page 109)

Be sure each ingredient used is completely milk-, egg-, and nut-free
(see pages 13-15)

20-Minute Pasta Dinner

Mad About Pasta (page 76) OR Pasta Bella (page 78)
(Purchased) dairy-, egg-, and nut-free Fresh Bread
or Rolls

30-Minute Family Favorite

Springtime Chicken Rotini (page 84)
Applesauce

LUNCH
Not Another Sandwich

Tantalizing Turkey Wraps (page 60)
Fresh fruit

Soup and Salad

Mexican Mini-Meatball Soup (page 28)
Tossed Green Salad with Tomato Vinaigrette (page 34)

Something Different

Curried Tuna Pockets (page 117)
Fresh Fruit Salad
Dairy-free Potato Chips

Be sure each ingredient used is completely milk-, egg-, and nut-free
(see pages 13-15)

Glossary

Al dente: Italian term used to describe pasta cooked until tender but slightly firm to the bite.

Bake: To cook, covered or uncovered, by dry heat (usually in an oven). When applied to meats, poultry, and vegetables cooked uncovered, the process is called roasting.

Beat: To stir or mix rapidly in a quick, even, circular motion, to make a mixture smooth, lighter, or fluffier. When using a spoon or wire whisk, lift mixture up and over with each stroke.

Blend: To thoroughly combine two or more ingredients until smooth and uniform in texture, color, and flavor.

Broil: To cook by direct heat in the broiler of an electric or gas range.

Chop: To cut food into small pieces.

Coat: To cover a food with a surface layer of another ingredient, such as flour, by sprinkling, dipping, or rolling.

Combine: To stir together two or more ingredients until blended.

Core: To remove the center of a fruit or vegetable.

Cream: To beat with a spoon or an electric mixer until soft, smooth, and fluffy, as in blending margarine and sugar.

Cut in: To distribute solid fat, such as margarine, into dry ingredients with a pastry blender until particles are the desired size.

Fold in: To incorporate a delicate substance into another substance. A rubber spatula is used to gently bring part of the mixture from the bottom of the bowl to the top. The process is repeated, while slowly rotating the bowl, until the ingredients are blended.

Grease and flour pan: A process for coating a baking pan in order to prevent the finished baked good from sticking to the pan. Using a folded napkin or paper towel, coat the entire inside surface of the pan with the specified "grease" (such as vegetable shortening). Then place a spoonful of flour in the baking pan. Shake the pan to coat the entire inside surface with a fine layer of flour, then shake out any excess flour from the pan.

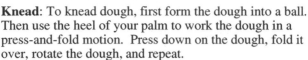

Knead: To knead dough, first form the dough into a ball. Then use the heel of your palm to work the dough in a press-and-fold motion. Press down on the dough, fold it over, rotate the dough, and repeat.

Marinade: To soak food in a (usually acidic) liquid in order to tenderize the food or to enhance its flavor.

Mince: To chop or cut food into very small pieces.

Packed brown sugar: Brown sugar is measured by tightly "packing" the sugar into the measuring cup. Use the back of a spoon to tightly press the brown sugar into the specified size measuring cup.

Poach: To cook very gently in hot liquid kept either just below or at the boiling point.

Preheat: To heat oven to desired temperature before beginning to cook.

Puree: To mash foods until perfectly smooth, usually by whirling in a blender or food processor.

Sauté: To cook food in a pan in a small quantity of hot oil, usually stirring frequently during the cooking process.

Simmer: To cook in liquid just below the boiling point. The surface of the liquid should be barely moving, broken from time to time by slowly rising bubbles.

Steam: To cook in water vapors, on a rack or in a steam basket above boiling water, in a covered pot or pan.

Toss: To combine ingredients with a lifting motion.

Index

A Request

Dear Reader,

I sincerely hope that you, your family, and your friends enjoy the recipes that are in this book. I know how challenging it is to cope with multiple food allergies. My deep desire to help others to meet these challenges has been my motivation in seeing this project through to completion.

I would love to hear from you!

Please send me your comments and feedback on *What's to Eat? The Milk-Free, Egg-Free, Nut-Free Food Allergy Cookbook.*

I can be reached at:

Linda Coss
Plumtree Press
P.O. Box 1313
Lake Forest, CA 92609-1313

or via e-mail:
LindaCoss@FoodAllergyCookbook.com

Thank you!

Order Information

What's to Eat? The Milk-Free, Egg-Free, Nut-Free Food Allergy Cookbook makes a great gift for your family and friends. If you have borrowed this copy from a friend or library, now is the time to order a copy for yourself, too!

To Order:

1. Photocopy and then fill out the order form on the reverse side of this page, or visit our website at:

   www.FoodAllergyBooks.com

2. Make check payable to Plumtree Press

3. Send completed order form with check or money order (in U.S. dollars only) to:

   Plumtree Press

   P.O. Box 1313, Dept. B

   Lake Forest, CA 92630-1313

4. Books will be shipped via U.S. mail.

5. If you have any questions, please send them to the above address or to: info@FoodAllergyBooks.com

Order Form

Note: Books can also be ordered via credit card from
www.FoodAllergyBooks.com

Please **photocopy** this form, fill it out, and mail it with payment
(in U.S. dollars only) to:

Plumtree Press
P.O. Box 1313, Dept. B
Lake Forest, CA 92609-1313

Qty	Book Title	Each	Total
	What's to Eat? The Milk-Free, Egg-Free, Nut-Free Food Allergy Cookbook	$16.95	
	How To Manage Your Child's Life-Threatening Food Allergies	$16.95	
	SUBTOTAL		
	Sales Tax: CA residents add 7.75% tax		
	Shipping and Handling $3.00/1 book or $4.50/2 books for U.S. Media Rate (3rd class) mail $5.00/1 book or $7.50/2 books for U.S. Priority Mail or Canadian orders $10.00/1 book or $15.00/2 books for shipments to other countries		
	TOTAL:		

Note: Prices and availability subject to change without notice.

Name: _____

Address: _____

_____

E-mail (optional): _____

June 2004